PSALMS OF THE JEWISH LITURGY

A Guide to their Beauty, Power, and Meaning

A New Translation & Commentary
in Memory of David L. Lieber

by
Miriyam Glazer

AVIV PRESS

NEW YORK

Library of Congress Cataloguing-in-Publication Data

Glazer, Miriyam, 1945–
    Psalms of the Jewish liturgy : a guide to their beauty, power, and meaning : a new translation & commentary in memory of David L. Lieber / by Miriyam Glazer
        p. cm.
    ISBN 978-0-916219-41-3 (alk. paper)
    1. Bible. O.T. Psalms–Commentaries.   2. Bible. O.T. Psalms–Liturgical use.   3. Bible. O.T. Psalms–Devotional use. I. Lieber, David L.   II. Bible. O.T. Psalms English. 2008.   III. Title.
    BS1430.53.G63   2008
    223'.2077–dc22   2008028769

Published by Aviv Press
An imprint of the Rabbinical Assembly
2080 Broadway, New York, NY 10027

Cover design by Rebecca Neimark

PRINTED IN THE UNITED STATES OF AMERICA

אָנָּה יְהֹוָה ... פִּתַּחְתָּ לְמוֹסֵרָי:

O *Adonai* . . . You loosened my bonds

(Psalm 116)

In memory of David L. Lieber,
beloved teacher and inspiration
and for A.E., who understands

Contents

The first number after each Psalm refers to the page on which the commentary appears, and the second, *italicized* number to the English translation.

Acknowledgements   ix

1. *Introduction:* Holy Reading   1

2. *"The Whole World and All that Is in It"*:
   The Psalms for the Days of the Week   14
        Sunday — Psalm 24   17, *31*
        Monday — Psalm 48   20, *33*
        Tuesday — Psalm 82   21, *35*
        Wednesday — Psalm 94   22, *37*
        Thursday — Psalm 81   24, *41*
        Friday — Psalm 93   26, *43*
        Shabbat—Psalm 92   28, *45*

3. *"You Turned My Grief into Dancing"*:
   Psalm 30 for Every Morning   46

4. *Falling on Your Face: Taḥanun*   50
        Psalm 6   51, *55*
        Psalm 130   52, *57*

5. *"I Bless Your Name Forever and Ever"*:
   The Daily Hallel   58
       Psalm 145   59, *71*
       Psalm 146   63, *75*
       Psalm 147   65, *77*
       Psalm 148   69, *81*
       Psalm 149   69, *83*
       Psalm 150   69, *85*

6. *Ecstatic Salvation*:
   The Psalms of the Festival Hallel   86
       Psalm 113   87, *91*
       Psalm 114   88, *93*
       Psalm 115   88, *95*
       Psalm 116   88, *97*
       Psalm 117   88, *99*
       Psalm 118   *101*

7. *Frolicking with Leviathan:* Rosh Hodesh   104
       Psalm 104   104, *107*

8. *A Heart of Flesh, a Heart of Courage*:
   Psalm for the Season of Repentance   112
       Psalm 27   112, *115*

9. *Glowing in the Nuptial Light*:
   The Psalms of Kabbalat Shabbat   118
       Psalm 95   119, *135*
       Psalm 96   126, *137*
       Psalm 97   128, *139*
       Psalm 98   130, *141*
       Psalm 99   131, *143*
       Psalm 29   132, *145*

Contents

10. *Starry Heavens, Moral Law:*
     Shabbat Morning's "Verses of Song"   146
         Psalm 19   148, *161*
         Psalm 34   151, *163*
         Psalm 90   153, *167*
         Psalm 91   155, *171*
         Psalm 135   156, *175*
         Psalm 136   156, *179*
         Psalm 33   157, *183*

11. *Reaping in Joy:* The Blessing After Meals   186
         Psalm 126   186, *193*

12. *"For the Sake of My Comrades and Friends":*
     A Psalm for Peace   194
         Psalm 122   194, *122*

13. *For You Are with Me:* Psalm 23   198
         Psalm 23   198, *201*

14. *Afterword*   202

Sources   205

List of Abbreviations   207

Acknowledgements

How This Book Came to Be:

The Psalms Class and Dr. David L. Lieber^{z"l}

Several years ago, as a student in rabbinical school, I took a course called *Psalms of the Liturgy* taught by Professor of Bible David L. Lieber^{z"l}, the President Emeritus of the American Jewish University (formerly University of Judaism), where I, too, have been a professor—in my case, of Literature—for what is now over twenty years. I had been a lover of the psalms most of my life—soaring with some, weeping with others, singing them robustly during services, turning to them in times when it felt as if "my cup runneth over" with joy, as well as in times of turmoil and great emotional pain. During synagogue services, while the rest of the congregation might be whizzing through the Shabbat morning "introductory psalms" before *Shaḥarit*, the Morning Service, I, most often, would fasten on one and spend the whole of that portion of the service mulling it over, line by line, letting myself truly feel it, truly enter it, truly make it my own. How is "*Adonai* . . . support for all who fall . . . raiser of all the subjugated," as we claim in the *Ashrei* (Ps 145)? What does it mean to say, "*Adonai* is close to those whose hearts are broken/and those whose spirits are crushed?" (Ps 34), I would ask myself.

In Dr. Lieber's class, there were no grandiose theological statements, no generalities. Instead, under Dr. Lieber's tutelage, we went over the psalms of the liturgy word-by-word, line-by-line, confronting grammatical and linguistic ambiguities, probing the intricate nuances of the Hebrew language, paying attention to the formal ways the psalms were structured. The scope of Dr. Lieber's learning truly awed us. For me, the process was pure joy: it was like discovering the finely and carefully wrought foundation stones of the home you have lived in with great pleasure for many years.

Some time after my rabbinical ordination, Dr. Lieber approached me. The *ḥumash* on which he had labored for many years as general editor, *Etz Ḥayim*, was finished, and he was eager to be involved in a new project. Would I want to collaborate on a new translation, commentary, and guide to the psalms of the Jewish liturgy?

Honored by his request and eager to work with Dr. Lieber, I was also thrilled. Here, at last, would be the opportunity to share with others what I had long felt, a feeling that deepened and was enriched in that Psalms class: the beauty, power, and meaning of these beloved poem-prayers. Our original idea was simply to produce pamphlets for use in the synagogue for the various psalm-series: something congregants could turn to during, say, the *Kabbalat Shabbat* services or *Hallel*. But then a colleague urged us to make a book. She realized that if it were in book form, readers could pore over it at their leisure at home, allowing them to deepen their own spiritual practice, as well as allowing the Jewish liturgy to become more alive for them.

Dr. Lieber shared his formal analyses of the themes and structures of the psalms with me, and with a fine-tooth comb (and occasionally, brutal honesty) went over my translations and commentaries, which I had based on my own insights and those I had gained in the Psalms class and through the material he shared with me. We worked slowly and as the years went by, along the way, Dr. Lieber passed the project entirely into my hands. It is clear to me, though, that without the learning Dr. Lieber shared—and I was only one of his many students over the years—and without his inspiration and encouragement and without his own love for this material—this book would never have come to be.

Dr. Lieber initiated and inspired the book. But, in honor of Dr. Lieber, it was Dr. Robert Wexler and friends of the American Jewish University, who enabled it to come into being. I want to acknowledge the generosity of Bruce Whizin, as well as of Bonnie and Mitchell S. Bloom; Joan Borinstein; Irma and Benjamin Breslauer and the Samuel and Helen Soref Foundation; Louis L. Colen; Janet and Jake Farber; Sharon and Herbert Glaser; Dorreta and Jona Goldrich; Lois and Richard Gunther; Lela and Dr. Norman Jacoby; Eleanor and Mark Lainer; Serene and Rubin M. Lazar; Mel Levine and Connie Bruck; Dena and Irving Schechter and the Hyman Levine Foundation; Judith and Louis Miller; Joy and Jerry Monkarsh; Heidi and Jon Monkarsh; Julie and Marc Platt; Jeanne and Anthony Pritzker; Marilyn and Stan Ross; Claudia and Sandor Samuels; Annette and Leonard Shapiro; Judith and S. Jerome Tamkin; Jeff Trenton; Mickey and Judge Joseph Wapner; Ruth Ziegler, and Marilyn Ziering.

I have several other very special people to thank. Professor Maeera Shreiber, my dear friend and colleague, pored over so many translations with me and shored up my confidence; my dear *havruta* Marshall Kramer not only read part of the manuscript but helpfully shared it with David Wilkof, who took the time to give me valuable, detailed feedback, most of which I adopted; Martin S. Cohen, whose own book, *Our Haven and our Strength: The Book of Psalms,* was a great help to me; and Rabbi Joel Rembaum, who offered me a very detailed, helpful critique of the initial version of the *Kabbalat Shabbat* commentary.

I am grateful for the editorial support of the editorial director of Aviv Press, Amy Gottlieb, and for the technical expertise, patience, and creativity of rabbinical student Adam Stein, who designed and set the Hebrew type.

Most of all, I want to express my deep gratitude to my husband, Rabbi Anthony Elman, who, with his characteristic wisdom and his constant love, encouraged and inspired me to give this project the passion and devotion I so longed to give.

CHAPTER ONE

Introduction:

Holy Reading

"Atem eydai n'um Hashem, v'ani El." You are my witnesses, says God, and I am God. Says Rabbi Shimon bar Yoḥai . . . [the line means] "If you are my witnesses, I am God. If you are not my witnesses, I am not God." (Sifre Deut 33:5)

Sometimes during services, we race through them. Sometimes we sing them to robust melodies. What we all too often *don't* succeed in doing during our religious services is to truly *experience* the psalms of our liturgy in their pathos, their power, their joyous exuberance, their vivid imagery, spiritual beauty, their utter majesty.

Yet, in the words of David L. Lieber, "the Book of Psalms, arguably the most beautiful collection of religious prayer poetry ever compiled, is second only to the Torah in its impact on the Jewish heart, mind, and spirit." Modern scholars believe the psalms were composed over many centuries, possibly by priests or Levites who worked in the Temple. According to Jewish tradition, however, the psalms were composed by King David, the "sweet singer of Israel"—and indeed, the psalms express as richly varied an emotional and spiritual terrain as does the biblical story of King David himself. The psalms are infused with joy, love, awe, ecstasy, and hope—as well as with grief, fear, anxiety, rage, and pain. "Sing a new song to *Adonai*, Who has worked wonders!" the psalmist beckons us (Ps 98). Or gazing out at the hills—perhaps at a nimble gazelle—proclaims, "How great are Your works, *Adonai*: everything made with such wisdom!" (Ps 104). Expressing a very different mood come words struggling for courage:

> *Adonai* is my light and my help, whom should I fear?
> *Adonai* is my source of strength, who can frighten me? (Ps 27)

Or needing to feel heard:

> Out of the depths I am calling to You, *Adonai*—O *Adonai*, hear
>   my voice—let Your ears truly hear the sound of my plea—
>   (Ps 130)

A haunting plaintiveness is woven into the psalm of *Taḥanun* ("Supplications"), the section of the daily service which grapples with our own shortcomings:

> *Adonai*, do not reject me out of anger or punish me in rage—
>   Be gentle with me, *Adonai*, for I am feeling such despair. . . .
>   (Ps 6)

whereas the *Ashrei*, traditionally recited three times every day, expresses a confident sense of the Holy One's bountiful generosity:

> They celebrate Your vast goodness endlessly, singing with joy of
>   Your tender acts . . .
> Opening Your hand, satisfying the desire of all living creatures . . .
>   (Ps 145)

From sorrow to joy, despair to ecstasy, fear to wonder, awe, and amazement; the psalms included in the Jewish liturgy span an immense emotional and spiritual terrain. Let's look at where in the liturgy they are found.

Psalms in the Siddur

To begin with, the Jewish prayer book, the siddur, includes a psalm for each day of the week, each of which has its own emotional tone. A glorious series of psalms welcomes the Shabbat on Friday night (Pss 95-99; 29), following a practice initiated in the sixteenth century in Safed, a town in northern Israel, where the kabbalistic mystics, dressed in white, went out to the hillside on the eve of Shabbat to welcome Shekhinah, the Divine Presence.

On Shabbat morning, a wide variety of psalms is recited as part of the *Pesukei Dezimra*, the "preliminary service," and ever since ancient times, the series called "The [Daily] Hallel" (Pss 145-150) is recited by observant Jews *every* morning to "warm up" before *Shaharit*, the Morning Service. Special days have their own special psalms. Hanukkah and the festivals of Passover, Shavuot, and Sukkot— as well as Israeli Independence Day, in some congregations—are marked by singing and reciting the psalms of victory and celebration called the "Festival Hallel" (Pss 113-118). Even Rosh Hodesh, the celebration of the new month on the Hebrew calendar, has its own psalm (104), along with a shortened version of the Festival Hallel.

Beginning in *Elul*, the month of soul-searching before Rosh Hashanah, we recite Ps 27, a gripping psalm of faith, every day until Yom Kippur or in some synagogues, until the end of Sukkot. On our festivals and festive occasions, as well as on every Shabbat, we preface the *Birkat Hamazon*, the Grace after Meals, with Ps 127. There are grief-stricken yet hopeful psalms, 49 and 42, recited during a *shivah* minyan, in a house of mourning. And there is what is perhaps the most well-known and beloved psalm of all, Ps 23, in which countless generations of mourners have found comfort.

Getting to truly know the great range of the psalms of the liturgy, allowing ourselves to *feel* them, to *experience* them, to *enter deeply into them,* is an adventure for the heart, mind, and soul. To begin with, the psalms offer such a vividly variegated range of qualities for God that our whole understanding of God-liness expands. For the psalmist, for example, the Holy One is at once royal, majestic, tender, compassionate, loving, healing, eternally just, *and* capable of great rage. The same God who hurls hailstones across the sky and "hangs the heavens as if they were drapes" (Ps 104) also "protects the outsider," and "helps widows and orphans stand on their feet" (Ps 146). The same God who makes sure that baby birds are fed also hitches a ride on the wings of the wind and frolics with Leviathan! (Pss 147; 104).

For the psalmist, *Adonai* is at once both universal and the Guardian and Restorer of Israel, in particular. The whole earth is called upon to rejoice in the existence of the God Who named every star in the universe and is the source of healing for *all* who are heartbroken, *all* who are oppressed. At the same time, *Adonai* has an intimate, loving, protective relationship with the people Israel:

When *Adonai* restored Zion, we were like dreamers.
Then our mouths were full of laughter—our tongues with songs
    of joy. (Ps 126)

Through this rich portrayal of the brilliant range of the quali-ties of the Holy One, the psalms offer us a renewed sense of inti-macy with the many different moods and phases of our own souls. To accept the infinite aspects of the One can open us to see and experience the many potential sides of ourselves. Gener-ous, kind, fierce about justice, angry, playful, loving, sturdy, the Creator of the universe and of all life, *as well as* the Guardian of Israel, the God depicted in the psalms can open us up to the hid-den or unarticulated nooks and crannies of our own being.

For example, some of the psalms of the liturgy have the capac-ity to awaken and to deepen our sense of awe at the marvels of our beautiful planet: the mountains and the hills, the rivers and the seas, the birds in the sky, the animals of the forest; the bolts of lightning that ignite the sky, the raging wind, the plants that provide us with food. Other psalms offer us a language to express the brokenness of our own hearts and to name the longings within us, whether they are longings for love, for faith, for wholeness, for peace, for understanding, for justice, for joy.

Part of the power of the psalms, moreover, is that they *are* and have been for centuries, poem-prayers of our collective experience. Thus even when we might be overcome by a deeply private grief and find ourselves turning to the words of Psalm 6:

> *Adonai*, do not reject me out of anger or punish me in rage—
> Be gentle with me, *Adonai*, for I am feeling such despair—(Ps 6)

we have the quiet comfort of knowing that we are not alone. We are in company with the millions of people who have ever lived in all corners of the world who, like us, have found solace in the very same words we are reciting now. The words of the psalm glisten with the spiritual energy of the ages.

For each of us as individuals, the psalms of the liturgy offer a vocabulary for our victories and our failures, a way in which to express the sheer intensity of life itself. They give voice to our sense of gratitude, as well as to our rage at injustice, cruelty, and violence. In ways that may startle and disconcert our more self-conscious—and thus perhaps more timid—modern sensibilities, the psalms acknowledge the reality of evil in the world and the existence of enemies for whose erasure they unequivocally call. Yet the psalms of the liturgy also beckon us to affirm that although we live in a troubled, conflicted, and at times chaotic world, and even though the human heart itself may be pierced by suffering and confusion, the God of the Jewish tradition offers us the promise of transformation. Whatever we may be going through, there is an ultimate order, an ultimate stability, and a promise of ultimate justice and benevolence upon which we can truly rely. In the words of the psalmist, "*Adonai* reigns!" (Psalm 97):

I celebrate You, *Adonai,* for You drew me up . . .
Adonai, my God, I cried out to You and You healed me. . . .
You turned my mourning into dancing, You freed me from my
    sackcloth,
You dressed me in joy—
Now my whole being sings Your glory. . . . (Ps 30)

God as Sovereign

Still: the psalms are ancient prayer-poems from a very different
world than ours. Inevitably, then, in the process of making the
psalms our own, some real barriers arise for many of us. One barrier may be especially present for us Americans, who are unac-
customed to accepting, or even contemplating, images rooted in
monarchy. But images of God as Sovereign of the universe are
vital to the psalmist as a way of describing God's role, as well as
the fact that this is ultimately an ordered and a just world. The
Kabbalat Shabbat psalms (Pss 95-99, Ps 29), for example,
depend for their very power on the welcoming of God as
monarch of the universe:

Adonai reigns! Before God's throne
nations tremble and the land quakes! (Ps 99)

But if the notion of a "sovereign" makes us uncomfortable, it
may be because what we are really visualizing is the simplistic
image of God as an old man with a long white beard. For the
psalmist, however, at the heart of the insistence that "*Adonai*
reigns!" is the profound faith that despite whatever chaos may
surround us, ultimately our world is ruled by an impalpable *ruah
hakodesh,* a transcendent spirit of lovingkindness, justice, and
holiness. Despite the reality of terrible evil, despite the chaos and
bloodshed that all-too-often beset human life, and despite
human suffering; in the view of the psalms, it is because *Adonai*
reigns that we can trust that justice and goodness *will* triumph in
the end. To believe that God is "sovereign of the universe" is to

have the faith that, if not in our own lives than in the lives of the generations to come, the blessings of peace *will* indeed someday spread over the face of the earth.

The Psalmist's "Enemies"

Another barrier, one that I alluded to above, may arise from the psalmist's frequent acknowledgement of personal, as well as collective "enemies." This comes partly from the psalmist's psychological vocabulary: sometimes it is clear that what the psalmist is calling an "enemy" is what we would call a barrage of anxiety, a sense of being overwhelmed by those soul-shaking inner voices of self-doubt, fear, and trembling. In Ps 6, for example, the speaker is filled with anguish and despair, going to bed night after night crying—so much so that the bed itself is "flooded with . . . tears, drenched in . . . weeping." But mid-way through the psalm comes a radical turning point, an experience of profound relief: "*Adonai* has heard the sound of my weeping! *Adonai* has heard my plea! *Adonai* accepts my prayer!" calls the psalmist, who goes on to say "My enemies will be alarmed and ashamed . . ." It is clear that those "enemies" are not warriors at the gates, but *inner demons*—the demons of illness, fear, terror, depression, pain, all of which scatter when relief and hope arrive.

On the other hand, when the psalmist says, for example, "kings conspired and advanced together" against Zion (Ps 48), the image scarcely suggests a psychological or spiritual enemy. And so, it seems to me, if the psalms are to be meaningful for us in our own time—rather than just historical relics—we must ask ourselves as individuals, as Jews, and as human beings, who or what in our own time *are* our enemies. What are the forces of evil in *our* world? Given the bloody history of the twentieth century and the still unfolding but already troubled history of the twenty-first, the psalmist's insistence on the reality of external "enemies" reminds us that we can't ignore the life-destroying forces that have plagued and still plague our world. At times those forces have been subtle: ways of thinking, ways of behaving, ways of regarding and treating our fellow human beings that erode the possibility of true justice and peace. But all too often in our time, "enemies" have been brazen, bloodthirsty, and cruelly destructive on a scale much vaster than any the ancient psalmist could have even begun to fathom. It may initially abrade our modern spiritual sensibilities to name those forces so baldly as "enemies"—but how else can we honestly identify human evil?

Translating the Psalms

Finally, of course, there is the question of language itself. The psalms are obviously, above all, Hebrew poems, Hebrew hymns, Hebrew prayers. They draw for their power and rhythm on the vocabulary and literary techniques of ancient Hebrew poetry, itself influenced by the hymns and poetry of the surrounding cultures.[1] Every word of the psalms, every image, every phrase, can be translated in so many different ways. In order to decide the particular English word to choose for a particular Hebrew one, the translator must be very clear about the *purpose* of the translation. For example, a translator might seek to be literally accurate if the intended audiences are linguists or biblical scholars. Or one might translate with the goal of rendering in English the specific literary techniques of the Hebrew, such as finding equivalents for the parallelisms on which the psalms often depend. In the end, translating the psalms involves many, many choices.

The nemesis of any translation, however, is depending upon formulaic words and phrases that, although technically accurate, are simply unbeautiful. The difficulty with phrases such as

---

[1] For a fine and concise description of the literary techniques of the psalms, as well as of the challenges they pose to a translator, see Robert Alter, *The Book of Psalms: A Translation with Commentary* (New York: Norton, 2007), pp. xiii–xxxix.

"righteous law" or "righteous judgment" or "steadfast love," as well as legal terminology such as "ordinances," "decrees," and "statutes" is not their lack of accuracy—it is *because* of their technical accuracy that so many translators have depended upon them for so many years. The difficulty with this terminology is that it lacks aesthetic, spiritual, and emotional resonance for most of us. The words and phrases bypass our spirit and fall with a thud; they feel lifeless.

Without watering down the challenges posed by the Hebrew, I sought to render the psalms of the liturgy into an English that enables them to be vividly accessible prayer-poems and hymns in their own right. That means seeking to render the beautiful, soulful Hebrew into beautiful, soulful English; trying to convey the inner sense, the feeling, the experience of a word or a line, if not its literal meaning. Ideally, it means seeking to do for the rest of the psalms of the Jewish liturgy what four hundred years ago a group of biblical scholars commissioned by King James of England managed to do for the twenty-third psalm. Scholars dispute the accuracy of some of its phrases. But when we recite the twenty-third psalm at a *Yizkor* (Memorial) service or at a funeral, which of the following is more moving?

Though I walk through a valley of deepest darkness,

or

Even though I walk through the darkest valley[2]

or

Yea, though I walk through the valley of the shadow of death.

[2]From *Tanakh: The Holy Scriptures, The New JPS Translation According to the Traditional Hebrew Text* (Philadelphia: JPS, 1985) and *The New Oxford Annotated Bible* (Oxford: Oxford University Press, 2001).

Which line enables one to feel more hope?

> Only goodness and steadfast love shall pursue me all the days of
> my life

or

> Surely goodness and mercy shall follow me all the days of my life.

Despite its archaic phrases and its gendered language, the King James Version of the twenty-third psalm is still as tender, as comforting, as calming and as inspiring, and as truly beloved, as it was centuries ago. Contemporary Jews might be uncomfortable by the use of "Lord" for *Adonai*; by the repetition of "He;" and by verb endings like "eth" ("*leadeth* me," "*maketh* me," "my cup *runneth* over"). Scholars might argue over the phrase "valley of the shadow of death," rather than, perhaps, "dark valleys." But just as the phrase "my cup runneth over" has entered our culture as a way of describing the experience of plenitude, of unbounded goodness, of utter joy, so, too, has the psalm as a whole become part of our cultural and spiritual inheritance. Though we will return to the psalm later in the book, moving through it in detail, I want to offer the King James version here, as well, in its entirety:

> The Lord is my shepherd; I shall not want.
> He maketh me lie down in green pastures: he leadeth me beside
> the still waters.
> He restoreth my soul: he leadeth me in the paths of righteousness
> for his name's sake.
> Yea, though I walk through the valley of the shadow of death, I
> will fear no evil: for thou art with me; thy rod and thy staff,
> they comfort me.
> Thou preparest a table before me in the presence of mine
> enemies: thou anointest my head with oil; my cup runneth
> over.
> Surely goodness and mercy shall follow me all the days of my life;
> and I will dwell in the house of the Lord forever.

The power and beauty of this translation result from a paradox: we do not experience it *as* a translation. Rather, the King James version of the twenty-third psalm is a soulful, rhythmic English-language prayer-poem in its own right. *We can pray this psalm;* we can feel its resonance.

Therefore, as I translated the psalms of the Jewish liturgy, it was the language of the King James version of the twenty-third psalm that inspired me. I don't mean, of course, that I sought to echo either its archaisms or its gendered language. The words "run-neth" (or "leadeth" or "maketh") do not appear in the present book. Respecting my own sensibility, as well as that of many of us today, I also avoided all gender-specific language for God.[3] Rather, I mean that I have sought to honor the inner meaning and intent of the Hebrew original while trying to offer English versions that are equal to the Hebrew in their spiritual power. That is why readers will discover that the line-lengths also differ between the Hebrew and English versions of a psalm. Each language has its own rhythm—each *word* in each language has its own rhythm, its own beat. Moreover, Hebrew has a concision foreign to English—what Hebrew can say in two words, English can take five to say. In order to honor those differences of rhythm and structure, I have frequently found that one Hebrew line needs to be divided into two, three, or even four lines of English to remain true to the *English* language. (To facilitate comparison between the two, I've nevertheless numbered the lines of the English version to correspond to the equivalent lines in the Hebrew [rather than the number of the line in the actual English version alone].) For a very long time, we have needed English translations of the psalms that we can truly pray.[4]

[3]In this, I am following the precedent of my colleague, Martin Samuel Cohen, in *Our Haven and Our Strength: The Book of Psalms* (New York: Aviv Press, 2004). See also his description of the gender of the psalmists themselves (pages xiii–xiv).

[4]Please note that psalms that appear in more than one context in our liturgy, such as Psalm 92, will be featured here in only one, but readers are encouraged to turn back to it to complete a sequence.

In the end, though, even the most beautiful translation is not enough. "In order for our words to truly bring the Presence," said the rebbe of the Warsaw Ghetto, Rabbi Kalonymous Kalman Shapira, "the person praying must first reveal his own self in words." The psalmist gives us the words. Sometimes those words may carry us aloft with their spiritual fervor; sometimes they may puzzle and challenge us; sometimes they may give a local habitation and a name to the otherwise inchoate musings and emotions within us. In the pages ahead, as we move through the psalms of the Jewish liturgy, I pray that we all find special lines, images, moments, whole psalms that especially speak to us, that ignite and deepen our encounter with the Holy One, and thus also further the awakening of our own truest selves.

Holy Reading

"And then the word of *Adonai* came to him, saying 'What are you doing here, Elijah? . . . Go out and stand on the mountain before *Adonai,* for *Adonai* is about to pass by. Now, there was a great wind—so strong it was splitting mountains and smashing rocks into pieces . . . but *Adonai* was not in the wind. After the wind there was an earthquake, but *Adonai* was not in the earthquake. After the earthquake there was a fire, but *Adonai* was not in the fire. And after the fire came a still, small voice . . ." (1 Kgs 19: 10 ff)

For the psalmist, the power and presence of God are often felt most vividly in the most dramatic elements of nature: in the depths of the sea or the mountain peaks; in thunderstorms, and the rumbling of lightning bolts shattering the sky. Yet there is a paradox when we recite even the most dramatically-charged psalm. For us to *experience* the poetry of the psalm, to let its holy language truly shine through to our heart, we need to grow so quiet we can *hear* the sound the psalmist heard—not with our "actual" but with our "inner" ear.

Only in the quiet can we hear the "still, small voice" of the Holy One, speaking to us through the psalms.

In the synagogue, reciting the psalms is a communal experience, and the beauty of the psalms is inextricable from our sense of participating in holy community, from our sense of sharing.

But *praying* the psalms can be a richly intimate experience as well.

"Holy Reading" is a practice called *Lectio Divina* in Catholic tradition, and *keri'ah kedoshah* in Jewish Spiritual Practice, developed to deepen one's prayerful encounter with the psalms.

Here is an easily accessible version of the practice: Find a moment in your day, and a place, that will be free of interruption.

Pick a psalm—perhaps the psalm for the day, or one of the psalms from one of the psalm-series. Begin reading very slowly until you find a line that gets your attention, that puzzles you, or entrances you, or that seems to speak to you in a special way.

Let yourself rest with that line, repeat it to yourself, ponder it, savor it, roll it around in your mouth, your heart, your imagination.

Memorize the line slowly . . .

Free associate: what memories, thoughts, experiences, events, emotions, does the line evoke for you?

Draw.

Dance.

Or sit quietly, meditating, ruminating. Finally, read the psalm as a whole again.

CHAPTER TWO

"The Whole World and All That Is in It":

The Psalms for the Days of the Week

Here's a suggestion: very early in the morning, find a quiet place, a place without distractions. Once you've found the right spot, sit comfortably and close your eyes. Try to quiet your busy brain, letting the flotsam and jetsam of thoughts, worries, shopping lists, errands, flow through and then out. . . . Take a few deep, peaceful breaths.

And now: imagine yourself bounding up the sand-colored narrow roads of ancient Jerusalem very early one spring morning, a Sunday, about two thousand years ago. You pass sheep and goats grazing on the hillside, an occasional shepherd; fields of wild rosemary, roadside patches of bitter lettuce, mustard, and brilliant red poppies, bushes of pomegranates, groves of olive trees. Perhaps you pass other pilgrims on your way.

The closer you come to Jerusalem, the louder the music grows: the whole earth seems to echo with the chorus of cymbals, drums, trumpets, lutes that you hear. And . . . voices! You hear a whole choir singing! Now you know the rumors you heard back home must be true; because if from this hillside you can hear the music and singing of the Levites in the Temple, they really can be heard as far away as Jericho, too![5]

At last, you arrive at the great gates of the Temple, that awe-inspiring, sacred space, the center of worship at the center of the world. The extraordinarily rich and rhythmic music fills your ears: echoing all around you, ever louder, is a glorious symphony of clanging cymbals, sounding horns, the rapping of drums, the vibrating strings of the lutes and lyres and harps. You are transported; you sway with the sound—and then, wonder of wonders, you hear the Levites singing the first line of Ps 24, the psalm for the first day of the week.

Try murmuring the opening words of the psalm to yourself now, over and over again:

> The whole world and all that is in it belong to *Adonai* . . .

Open your eyes. Welcome to God's world and to the Psalms for the Days of the Week!

Working Our Way through the Week:

The Power of the Sequence

We may no longer have the Temple, or the ancient melodies of the Levites or their instrumental scores. But we do have the words to the psalms themselves, the very same words the Levites sang. If we take the time to enter into them, to mull them over, chant them for ourselves, make them our own, reciting this ancient sequence of seven psalms, one per day, can become a powerful— even a life-changing—experience.

The Mishnah tells us *which* psalm the Levites would recite each day (and to this day we recite the same ones in the same sequence). The Talmud expands the description in the Mishnah by offering us an explanation of *why*. According to Rabbi Yehu-

---

[5]The Mishnah says you can even hear the opening of the great gate of the Temple all the way to Jericho—along with the horns and drums and cymbals and the singing (Mishnah Tamid 3:8).

dah, who learned it from Rabbi Akiva, the sequence of the psalms of the week recapitulates the process of the creation of the world described in the opening pages of Genesis![6] For example, on Sunday, the first day of the week, we proclaim that "The whole world and all that is in it belong to *Adonai!*" (Ps 24) to honor the moment on the very first day that God created the universe and gave to it human beings. Similarly, the psalm for Monday, which begins, "Great is *Adonai*, and greatly praised, in the city of our God, on the holy mountain . . ." (Ps 48), refers to the second day of creation. One of the most delightful correspondences that the rabbis see is for Thursday, the fifth day, on which we recite Ps 81:

> Sing joyously to God, our source of strength, shout out to the
> God of Jacob!

According to the rabbis, because on the fifth day birds and fish were created, it is *they* who are joyously singing their little hearts out to God, blessing their Creator!

Challenges of the Week

Recapitulating the process of creation is just one way of looking at the weekly sequence of psalms. For a very different and demanding process is also working its way through the week— and it is one that undermines any possibility of complacency on our part. As we will see, we begin the week on Sunday by offering a robust, exhilarating welcoming of *Adonai* in our lives and our world. No sooner do we do that, though, than the psalms of the following days force us to face how unutterably *far* our world is from God—that is, from the way the world should be, from the way the world was *intended* to be. How riven with injustice our world is. How cruel it is. How tenuous human confidence and strength can be. When we get to the center of the week, Wednes-

---

[6]See BT, Rosh Hashanah 31a. ("BT" will be used throughout the book to refer to the Babylonian Talmud.)

day, the fourth day, we are right at the heart of the evil in the world, right at the heart of our own shortcomings.

A turning point from the anguish and anger comes on Thursday, the fifth day, when we get ever closer to Shabbat; "O Israel," God calls out, "if only you would hear Me!" By Friday, a true transformation has occurred—not only do we celebrate God's reign in our universe, but we declare our love for God's law, God's Way. By Shabbat morning, we have achieved a sense of spiritual and existential security and a reassuring, gentle, and beautiful promise. Going through the week, then, is like going through the fiery furnace of human life into the beauty of God's majestic light.

SUNDAY: PSALM 24

"The whole world and all that is within it belong to *Adonai*." With that line, we begin the week. Just as the rabbis taught that the sequence of these psalms recapitulates the creation of the world every week, so we can regard *every* beginning of a week not solely as a continuation of what we have already been, already done, already thought, and already felt, but rather as a *whole new beginning* in our ever-unfolding lives.

The very nature of the opening line reinforces that sense of an ever-new beginning. *The whole world and all that is within it belong to Adonai.* The more you think about it, the more amazing that declaration is! For the psalm is announcing that the skies above us and the galaxies billions of light years away from us are part of God's world—along with the people we love and the people we really don't like, the deer on our mountains, the ants and the ant-eater, the rivers, the rainbows, the hummingbird, the whale and the goldfish, the mosquito and the microbe, the disease-carrying virus, the TV, the industrial crane: *everything* is God's. What if, after reciting this psalm early Sunday morning, we let that opening line rest in no-motion in the back of our brain as we went through the day, or if intermittently we murmured it over and over again? How would it change our perceptions? How would it change our attitude toward the traffic on the freeway, the driver who just cut into our lane?

A World We Can Trust

The opening line of Ps 24 is evocative enough to sustain meditation for the whole day (and a whole lifetime!), yet the psalm has even more to offer us. For the psalmist immediately adds a second motif, one that recurs in many of the psalms. It is the idea that our world is "set . . . firmly"—that, thanks to the Creator, the earth we live on is secure. Deeply to believe that is so can offer our generation in particular a sense of existential reassurance, in the face of present anxieties about melting ice caps, global warming, tidal waves, expanding deserts, wildly destructive hurricanes, tornadoes that rip apart whole cities, and earthquakes that swallow thousands. Scientists know that we live in a universe of laws; similarly, the psalm reassures us that whatever natural upheavals we suffer, however our land may be tossed and shaken about, this is God's world and thus, it is ultimately stable and ultimately secure. Whether or not wars rage on earth, the earth will rotate on its axis; the moon will glow in the sky at night, and the sun will rise in the morning. We need not live in anxiety or fear. We can trust the ground we walk on.

Standing in God's Holy Place

But it is not enough to feel secure in our world, according to the psalmist. We have more to do with our lives: the spiritual challenge is to "ascend the mountain of *Adonai*." In ancient days, the "mountain of *Adonai*" and God's "holy place" in all likelihood were allusions to the Temple. But we have no Temple. So what does it mean today to *us* to "ascend the mountain of *Adonai?*" What does it mean to "stand in God's holy place?"

If we were in synagogue on Monday or Thursday morning for the Torah reading, we would be singing these words as the Torah is returned to the ark. It would be as if the ark itself is the "holy place," and all of us greeting the Torah as it is carried around the sanctuary en route to the ark are the pilgrims asking to accompany it.

But what if we are at home, quietly chanting the psalm by ourselves, to ourselves, on a Sunday morning?

Then "God's holy place" can become exactly where we are at the moment we are there: here, now. The "mountain of *Adonai*," "God's holy place," becomes the very place on which we "stand" the moment we honor our own moral selves: when we trust we are living lives of integrity, are honest with ourselves and honest with others—when we are living without subterfuge, obfuscation, defensiveness, false promises, excuses. Without lies. Without masks. Therefore, with no fear of being "found out," no worry about "what I should tell them," no need to "cover up," no barriers between who we say we are and who we truly are.

To live with "clean hands and a pure heart" is to be like Moses at the burning bush. God tells Moses to take off his shoes because the very ground on which Moses is standing is "holy ground." The psalm suggests to us that *every ground is holy ground, because the whole world and all within it is God's.* Isn't the psalm suggesting to us that to realize that fully, to realize fully the holiness on which we stand is to feel blessed?

Opening Our World — and Eyes — to God's Presence

The next section of the psalm is like the next turn of a magnificent dance. The psalm sought to move our moral selves to "God's holy place" and reaffirmed that we are a generation seeking God's presence; now it calls for opening up the very gates of our world to God. What are those "gates of the world?"

In ancient times, the image probably referred to the gates of the Temple. We are without the Temple—but we are not without the gates. In our day, one way to understand the gates is as the poet William Blake did: the gates of the world are what he called the "doors of perception." Just as "the whole world" is

God's, and everywhere we stand has the potential to be "holy ground," so, in Blake's words,

If the doors of perception were cleansed, everything would appear as it is: infinite.

There's a small rock on my desk which I picked up from a vast Alaskan glacier. Looking at the rock, I see, in my mind's eye, the awe-inspiring, vast, frozen glacier as a whole, along with a universe eons of ages old with its ancient minerals, its freezings and meltings, its expanding and contracting. Seeing the rock this way is like seeing "a world in a grain of sand, heaven in a wildflower." The rock becomes a gate to the whole world. And so it is with every rock and every leaf, every cell, or nucleus of a cell under a microscope. Every smile, every hug, every handshake, every act of kindness, every honest sharing is a "gate of the world," for it has the potential to evoke a sense of wonder and an opening of our hearts to the Divine. It is a perception of God's presence in everything in the world, a perception of the infinite in the finite. Thus every "gate of the world" also becomes a "gate to eternity." From this point of view, the psalm suggests to us that when we rid ourselves of falsity and when we allow ourselves to perceive one another and the world in which we live with our spiritual imaginations, the "God of Glory," "*Adonai*, God of the world," can enter our lives.

Not a bad way to begin the week.

MONDAY: PSALM 48

On the second day of creation, according to the Torah:

God said:
Let there be a dome amid the waters,
and let it separate waters from waters!
God made the dome
and separated the waters that were below the dome from the
    waters that were above the dome . . . God called the dome:
    Heaven! . . . (Gen 1:6–7)[7]

[7]*The Five Books of Moses: A New Translation with Introductions, Commentary, and Notes by Everett Fox* (New York: Schocken, 1995), p. 13.

Just as the book of Genesis tells us that on the second day God created heaven, so, as our ancient rabbis teach us, on the second day of our week we recite Ps 48 to celebrate the creation of Jerusalem and its heart, Mount Zion. What is most striking about the psalm's depiction of Mount Zion is its emphasis on both its beauty and its strength. Zion is the "delight of the earth, beautiful and high," and it is also the citadel of the nation of Israel, a place so awe-inspiring that those who would want to attack it flee the very moment they behold it.

In such a context, one might expect a celebratory phrase about God-as-Warrior, able to intimidate those conspiring kings who plan an attack on Zion. But no sooner does the psalm describe how the kings fled, then it goes on to speak of God's kindness, God's justice, and God's Torah. The suggestion, it seems to me, is that we are not really talking about an actual battle at all. Rather, the impulse for the psalm is a celebration of the three core aspects of our faith: God, Torah, and Zion, each of which incorporates justice, beauty, and truth. And the challenge it presents us with is having to ask ourselves: how do we incorporate justice, beauty, and truth into our lives on this day? On any day?

TUESDAY: PSALM 82

As we move further from the preceding Shabbat, and more closely into the center of the workaday week, the distance between the way things should be and the way they are becomes much more glaring. The psalms for Tuesday and Wednesday are perturbed, angry. Ps 82, the psalm for Tuesday, envisions God in a heavenly court admonishing the divine judges of the nations for ruling with cruelty rather than with kindness; favoring the mighty rather than the powerless. What is so remarkable here is an idea that we may take so for granted that we don't fully realize its mind- and world-altering power: the Ruler of the universe whom we celebrate, the Almighty God we honor, is the Divinity who stands up for the powerless, the poor, the needy, the destitute. What profound implications there are for our the insistence of our tradition on justice and fairness for the weak—on giving voice to the powerless, and protecting the needy! The psalm is claiming that the absence of justice in the world makes the world as a whole totter. Tuesday, today, would thus seem to be a perfect day to focus on what we as individuals can do to set the world right.

WEDNESDAY: PSALM 94

Wednesday: the day suspended between the Shabbat that has passed and the Shabbat that will be, and thus further from *any* Shabbat that a day can be. Perhaps that is why, of all the daily psalms, the psalm for Wednesday is the most *angry*, the most impassioned. In the book of Genesis, God creates the "lights in the dome of the heavens" and the "two great lights," sun and moon, on the fourth day. In our psalmist's vision, because demagogues and tyrants have taken control and the weak are suffering and dying at their hands, only the fierce light of God can make a difference now. This is a day of rage, a day on which to feel fully in one's innards the suffering of the victims of violence, war, exploitation, greed—suffering that has only intensified and spread since the day this psalm was written.

What makes this psalm even more powerful, even more poignant, is that it does not rest with its vivid and angry denunciation of the cruelty visited upon the weak by the strong. Nor does it rest with a call to God to punish them. Instead, it grows calmer, as if in an interlude. Focusing on Israel, it expresses the faith that one *can* trust that "justice will be restored." And then, in its moving third section, it becomes intensely personal, depicting, in what we might hear as a quiet, inwardly-oriented voice, the emotional power of a relationship with God in all its vulnerability.

Who will rise up with me against evildoers? asks the psalmist. The question seems to jump off the page. From the moment we murmur that line in prayer, we ourselves are called upon to ask whether *we* are among those who stand up. What would it mean for us, now and here, to do so? Who are the "evildoers" we are willing to stand up against—who are the ones we stand up against in our daily lives—and who are those that we ignore? What does "standing up to evildoers" mean for us? Protests? Checks sent to various organizations? Volunteer work? Letters to Editors? Speaking out wherever and whenever we see a miscarriage of justice, a cruel exploitation, wrongdoing of any kind? What is the ultimate source of the courage to stand up, to believe in, and to fight for justice, to "keep your eye on the prize?"

"If Adonai *were not my help, my soul would almost be silenced"*: for the psalmist, that ultimate source of courage is *Adonai*.

To have faith in *Adonai*, to seek closeness with a just, loving, and fair God, is at once the source of the passionate demand for justice in the world, and paradoxically, the source of calm in the eye of the storm, the way through the bewildering forest, the refuge in the war-zone, the Rock. After the fury expressed in the psalm, then, after the anxieties and the anger, comes this quieter voice of trust. The almost shocking final lines of the psalm are uttered with the voice of faith in the triumph of the good.

Ultimately, the psalmist asserts, the evil of the world will not be merely suppressed or just contained.

Ultimately the evil will be wiped out.

"Wiped out"? *Imagine what it would feel like to live in a world where those words had come true.*

THURSDAY: PSALM 81

"Sing joyously to God, our source of strength!"—Rabbi Yehudah, citing Rabbi Akiva, says that the Levites recited those opening words of Thursday's psalm because it was on the fifth day that God created the "birds and the fish to offer praise to God's

name" (BT, Rosh Hashanah, 31a). Perhaps the birds and fish did sing. The medieval sage Rashi says, though, that it's when we human beings see the vast variety of birds flying past us in the sky, that we are moved, surely, to praise the Creator!

I thought of Rashi's comment just a few days ago when my neighbor pointed out the beautiful little red woodpecker tapping away on the high branches of the tree in front of my house. I had never seen a woodpecker before, and the sight filled my eyes with delight. I laughed with pleasure. Then, truth be told, *because* Rashi's comment was so fresh in my mind, I found myself reciting the blessing for seeing creatures of great beauty:

ברוך אתה יהוה אלהינו מלך העולם שככה לו בעולמו

Praised are You, *Adonai* our God, Sovereign of the Universe, who has such beauty in Your world.

Later that day, I found myself wondering how often, really, it occurs to most of us first to notice, and then to express our pleasure and delight at seeing, say, a cardinal, a robin red-breast, or that sweetest of all creatures, a hummingbird, in our garden? And if we do, would we respond, as in *Pirkei Shirah*, with our own "joyous song" to God?

Given the opening lines to the psalm for Thursday, the fifth day seems a very good day on which to remind ourselves of how deeply good it feels to offer words of gratitude and joy to the Creator when we are blessed with a chance to experience the wonder and beauty of nature.

Because the psalm soon becomes much more complex, it may seem that such an expression of gratitude to God for the beauty of creation is just a peripheral theme of Ps 81. But indeed it isn't. For what Ps 81 captures is a state of ambivalence. To begin with, the ancient rabbis believed the reference of the psalm was to Rosh Hashanah, a "feast" day that is also at the

new moon. Later commentators argued that the psalm was originally written to celebrate Rosh Hodesh, the new moon; others,
translating "waxing moon" to mean "full moon," believe it refers
to Sukkot.[8] *Whatever* the occasion for the celebration evoked by
the opening lines of the psalm, however, the psalm itself both
*exhorts us to go all out in an ecstatic expression to God of our
joy*—beating our drums, strumming harps, singing out—and at
the same time *cautions us about how easy it is to lose a sense of
holiness*, a sense of God in our lives, to go astray, to go, as it
were, numb. The psalm implies strongly to us that we have
choices to make.

Coming on the brink of Erev Shabbat, the psalm for Thursday echoes the themes of the opening psalm of the *Kabbalat
Shabbat*, the psalm we often call *Lekhu Neranenah* ("Come let
us sing!"). But whereas the latter, Ps 95, ends with a recollection
of God's rage at the stubbornness of our ancestors in the wilderness, Ps 81 ends with an evocative promise.

There are the times—the "set times" like our festivals, and
also the personal times, the bat and bar mitzvahs, the weddings—when we truly "go all out" in our celebrations. With
music, dancing, feasting, in our joy we feel like we and all of our
guests are on God's path. With exuberance, we express our gratitude to God, just as in the opening of our psalm.

There are other times when we feel trapped or lost; when we
cry out "from the straits," and with immense relief, feel
answered. We feel terribly lonely, and the phone rings. We are
worried or fearful or overcome by anxiety, and calming news
comes. We worry about unemployment, and get the offer of a
job. We feel overwhelmed by problems and discover a solution,
or in the absence of a solution, a quiet that enables us to see our
way clear.

[8]See Adele Berlin and Marc Brettler, *The Jewish Study Bible* (New York: Oxford,
2004), p. 1374; and Alter, *The Book of Psalms*, p. 288.

But there are many other times when we are neither feasting nor sorrowing, neither ecstatic nor despairing. Instead, we're in between—in a "wilderness;"—when, in the words of Lawrence Kushner, "the everyday world seems strewn with rocks."[9] Rocks, not impassable boulders. The "quiet desperation" that can mark ordinary life. The "blahs," not despair. Just trudging on. The promise of this psalm is that, if we *don't* lose faith then, we *will* find spiritual nourishment. In the most ordinary of circumstances, in all the in-between times—in the very rocks that seem to obstruct, litter or slow our path, we have the possibility of discovering the "honey."[9]

So here we are, on Thursday. The workaday week is almost behind us, but not quite. Shabbat is almost here, but not quite.

Thursday itself *is an in-between time.*

What a good day to focus on imagining the taste on our lips, the taste in our souls, of God's finest wheat. God's golden honey.

FRIDAY: PSALM 93

On the sixth day of creation, God made "living creatures of every kind," wild animals, cattle, and all the creepy-crawlies. And when all other animals were made, God created *Adam*, the Human, crown of creation, stewards of all that God had created. The thirteenth century collection *Yalkut Shimoni* offers a lovely *aggadah*, a "legend," about this moment of creation. According to the *aggadah*, when Adam was first created, all the animals imagined that it was Adam who had created *them*. They came to bow down before this first human. Adam said: "Why are you bowing down to me? Come with me and together we'll bow down to the Creator of us all." At that moment, Adam opened

---

[9]See Lawrence Kushner, *Honey from the Rock: Ten Gates of Jewish Mysticism* (New York: Harper & Row, 1977), p. 14.

his mouth, calling *"Adonai* reigns, robed in majesty!" and all of creation responded, "the world is stable and will not be shaken!"

The beauty of this legend lies at least in part in its suggestion that when *we acknowledge God* as the sovereign of our world, *then* "God reigns robed in majesty." Rashi suggests that indeed it is that very acknowledgement that allows us to experience our world as profoundly and ultimately "stable." That experience of stability, moreover—that experience of a kind of majestic, awe-inspiring, still point in a whirlwind of chaos—is reinforced by the imagery of the lines that follow.

> Though the seas have risen, *Adonai,* the sound of the seas has risen, the pounding waves of the sea roar

> Stronger than the thundering water, mightier than the break-ers of the sea, is the majesty of *Adonai* on high.

Living just footsteps from the Atlantic shore during my child-hood, I remember how awestruck we were during hurricane sea-son when the lightning flashed, the thunder roared, rain poured down furiously as we huddled at a window in our dining room to watch the mightiness of the massive, roaring waves as they rose and broke not many feet from our house, pouring sea water down the street we lived on, down to the other end of the penin-sula, where the ocean water met the restive bay. Despite the ris-ing sea, the pounding waves, the thundering water, my sisters and I, all little girls then, nevertheless managed to feel safe, secure. First: the house we lived in—a big, sturdy, old beach house—had weathered many a storm in the past, and of course, we had full faith in our mom and dad and their ability to take care of us.

Transmuted to a theological plane, the psalm is suggesting to us that the spiritual equivalent of that sturdy old house of my childhood is our Torah. Torah is our *sacred* home, for its teaching, its way of life, gives us the most profound and unshakable sense of spiritual security whatever the tempests we face in our world. *It is a tree of life to those who hold fast to it,* as we sing in synagogue when we return the Torah scrolls to the ark. As we end the workaday week and prepare to enter the world of Shabbat, it is good to lay the tempests of daily life aside and stand with Adam and the rest of creation to celebrate the Creator of us all.

SHABBAT: PSALM 92

I often wonder what it was about the melody *of tzadik kata-mar yifrah — the just are as fertile as a date palm —* that made me fall in love with it as a child in my Shabbat morning Junior Congregation services at Temple Beth El of Rockaway Park all those years ago. Was it the way we lifted our voices high as we sang of that palm tree and cedar growing tall on Mount Lebanon, as if in a kind of onomatopoeia? We sing the words to the same melody today at the Library Minyan I attend, on the other side of the continent. And the melody still moves me — though now, over fifty years later, what is so soul-calming, so exhilarating about the psalm is, admittedly, less that lovely melody than the promise of the psalm that even in old age, if we are true and just, we will flourish. . . .

The Midrash suggests that Shabbat itself stood up and sang Ps 92 at the end of the first week of creation. Perhaps, millennia later, every week Shabbat *still* sings the psalm because Shabbat is both age-old and eternally new; it is also eternally fresh, flourishing, luxuriant. At the end of the week, it is good, it is healing, to assert, firmly, that evil in the world is not at all insurmountable, that evildoers are the easily-cut-down grass. And it is good, and it is healing, to assert with soaring voices that the life-force of goodness and righteousness, of alignment with the will of God, is eternally fresh, flourishing — and, like ever-growing palms, like cedars growing sky-ward on the mountain—luxuriant, even in old age.

At the very end of the week, how good to give thanks to *Adonai*.

SUNDAY: PSALM 24

הַיּוֹם יוֹם רִאשׁוֹן בַּשַּׁבָּת שֶׁבּוֹ הָיוּ הַלְוִיִּם אוֹמְרִים
בְּבֵית הַמִּקְדָּשׁ:

1   לְדָוִד מִזְמוֹר

לַיהוָה הָאָרֶץ וּמְלוֹאָהּ תֵּבֵל וְיֹשְׁבֵי בָהּ:

כִּי הוּא עַל־יַמִּים יְסָדָהּ וְעַל־נְהָרוֹת יְכוֹנְנֶהָ:

מִי־יַעֲלֶה בְהַר יְהוָה וּמִי־יָקוּם בִּמְקוֹם קָדְשׁוֹ:

5   נְקִי כַפַּיִם וּבַר לֵבָב אֲשֶׁר לֹא־נָשָׂא לַשָּׁוְא נַפְשִׁי וְלֹא
נִשְׁבַּע לְמִרְמָה:

יִשָּׂא בְרָכָה מֵאֵת יְהוָה וּצְדָקָה מֵאֱלֹהֵי יִשְׁעוֹ:

זֶה דּוֹר דֹּרְשָׁיו מְבַקְשֵׁי פָנֶיךָ יַעֲקֹב סֶלָה:

שְׂאוּ שְׁעָרִים רָאשֵׁיכֶם וְהִנָּשְׂאוּ פִּתְחֵי עוֹלָם
וְיָבוֹא מֶלֶךְ הַכָּבוֹד:

מִי זֶה מֶלֶךְ הַכָּבוֹד יְהוָה עִזּוּז וְגִבּוֹר יְהוָה גִּבּוֹר מִלְחָמָה:

10 שְׂאוּ שְׁעָרִים רָאשֵׁיכֶם וּשְׂאוּ פִּתְחֵי עוֹלָם וְיָבֹא מֶלֶךְ הַכָּבוֹד:

מִי הוּא זֶה מֶלֶךְ הַכָּבוֹד יְהוָה צְבָאוֹת הוּא מֶלֶךְ
הַכָּבוֹד סֶלָה:

SUNDAY: PSALM 24

Today is the first day of the week, when the Levites sang this
   psalm in the Temple:

1   *A David psalm.*
   The whole world and all that is within it belong to *Adonai,*
   the earth and all its inhabitants—
   For *Adonai* founded the earth on the seas,
   and on flowing streams set it firmly.

   Who ascends the mountain of *Adonai?* Who stands in God's
      holy place?

5   Those who have clean hands and a pure heart,
   who have not abased themselves by lying,
   nor made vows they never meant to keep.
   They shall feel blessed by *Adonai,*
   treated justly by a loving God.

   Like Jacob, this is a generation of seekers,
   a generation seeking Your presence.

10   Lift the gates of the world high!
   Let the gates to eternity be lifted high
   so the God of Glory can enter!
   Who is this God of Glory?
   Adonai, strong and heroic, *Adonai,* heroic in struggle—
   Lift the gates of the world high, lift the gates to eternity
   so the God of glory can enter!
   Who is this God of Glory? *Adonai,* God of the world,
      Adonai is God of Glory. Selah.

MONDAY: PSALM 48

הַיּוֹם יוֹם שֵׁנִי בַּשַּׁבָּת שֶׁבּוֹ הָיוּ הַלְוִיִּם אוֹמְרִים
בְּבֵית הַמִּקְדָּשׁ:

1   שִׁיר מִזְמוֹר לִבְנֵי־קֹרַח:

גָּדוֹל יְהוָה וּמְהֻלָּל מְאֹד בְּעִיר אֱלֹהֵינוּ הַר־קָדְשׁוֹ:

יְפֵה נוֹף מְשׂוֹשׂ כָּל־הָאָרֶץ הַר־צִיּוֹן יַרְכְּתֵי צָפוֹן קִרְיַת
מֶלֶךְ רָב:

אֱלֹהִים בְּאַרְמְנוֹתֶיהָ נוֹדַע לְמִשְׂגָּב:

5   כִּי־הִנֵּה הַמְּלָכִים נוֹעֲדוּ עָבְרוּ יַחְדָּו:

הֵמָּה רָאוּ כֵּן תָּמָהוּ נִבְהֲלוּ נֶחְפָּזוּ:

רְעָדָה אֲחָזָתַם שָׁם חִיל כַּיּוֹלֵדָה:

בְּרוּחַ קָדִים תְּשַׁבֵּר אֳנִיּוֹת תַּרְשִׁישׁ:

כַּאֲשֶׁר שָׁמַעְנוּ כֵּן רָאִינוּ בְּעִיר יְהוָה צְבָאוֹת בְּעִיר אֱלֹהֵינוּ
אֱלֹהִים יְכוֹנְנֶהָ עַד־עוֹלָם סֶלָה:

10   דִּמִּינוּ אֱלֹהִים חַסְדֶּךָ בְּקֶרֶב הֵיכָלֶךָ:

כְּשִׁמְךָ אֱלֹהִים כֵּן תְּהִלָּתְךָ עַל־קַצְוֵי־אֶרֶץ צֶדֶק מָלְאָה יְמִינֶךָ:

יִשְׂמַח הַר־צִיּוֹן תָּגֵלְנָה בְּנוֹת יְהוּדָה לְמַעַן מִשְׁפָּטֶיךָ:

סֹבּוּ צִיּוֹן וְהַקִּיפוּהָ סִפְרוּ מִגְדָּלֶיהָ:

שִׁיתוּ לִבְּכֶם לְחֵילָה פַּסְּגוּ אַרְמְנוֹתֶיהָ לְמַעַן תְּסַפְּרוּ
לְדוֹר אַחֲרוֹן:

15   כִּי זֶה אֱלֹהִים אֱלֹהֵינוּ עוֹלָם וָעֶד הוּא יְנַהֲגֵנוּ עַל־מוּת:

MONDAY: PSALM 48

Today is the second day of the week, when the Levites sang this
    psalm in the Temple:

1   A song, a psalm for the sons of Koraḥ.
     Great is *Adonai*, and greatly praised
     in the city of our God, on the holy mountain—
     the delight of the earth, beautiful and high: Mount Zion,
     where, in the distance, our great God dwells.
     God, the citadels of Zion are our refuge.

5   For look—when the kings assembled and advanced
        together and
        they saw it—
     they were astounded,
     overwhelmed,
     seized with trembling like a woman in labor—
     they fled like the east wind smashing the ships of Tarshish.
     What we once only heard of, now we have witnessed
        in the city of *Adonai*,
     the city of our God—may You preserve it forever!

10 God, in Your sanctuary we meditate on Your kindness:
     how Your name and Your praise reach to the ends of the
        earth
     and justice fills Your right hand.

     Let Mount Zion rejoice in your Torah! let the towns of Judah
        exult,
     and walk around Zion—walk all around her
     count her towers— turn your heart to her citadels
     climb up to her palaces
     so you can tell her story to generations to come:

15 For this is God, our God forever, the One Who will
        guide us
     forevermore.

TUESDAY: PSALM 82

הַיּוֹם יוֹם שְׁלִישִׁי בַּשַּׁבָּת שֶׁבּוֹ הָיוּ הַלְוִיִּם אוֹמְרִים
בְּבֵית הַמִּקְדָּשׁ:

1   מִזְמוֹר לְאָסָף אֱלֹהִים נִצָּב בַּעֲדַת־אֵל בְּקֶרֶב אֱלֹהִים יִשְׁפֹּט:

עַד־מָתַי תִּשְׁפְּטוּ־עָוֶל וּפְנֵי רְשָׁעִים תִּשְׂאוּ־סֶלָה:

שִׁפְטוּ־דָל וְיָתוֹם עָנִי וָרָשׁ הַצְדִּיקוּ:

פַּלְּטוּ־דַל וְאֶבְיוֹן מִיַּד רְשָׁעִים הַצִּילוּ:

5   לֹא יָדְעוּ וְלֹא יָבִינוּ בַּחֲשֵׁכָה יִתְהַלָּכוּ יִמּוֹטוּ כָּל־מוֹסְדֵי אָרֶץ:

אֲנִי אָמַרְתִּי אֱלֹהִים אַתֶּם וּבְנֵי עֶלְיוֹן כֻּלְּכֶם:

אָכֵן כְּאָדָם תְּמוּתוּן וּכְאַחַד הַשָּׂרִים תִּפֹּלוּ:

קוּמָה אֱלֹהִים שָׁפְטָה הָאָרֶץ כִּי־אַתָּה תִנְחַל בְּכָל־הַגּוֹיִם:

TUESDAY: PSALM 82

Today is the third day of the week, when the Levites sang this
psalm in the Temple:

1   *A psalm of Asaph.*
    God stands up in the heavenly council, rendering judgment
        in the midst of the gods:
    "How long will you judge unjustly and show favor to the
        wicked?
    You should show justice to the poor, the orphan, the
        beggars, the destitute—
    you should rescue the poor and needy from the clutches of
        the wicked."

5   But they know nothing, understand nothing, they walk
        about in darkness
    while the very foundations of the earth totter.
    "I once said you were divine, children of the Most High—all
        of you.
    But you will die like all humans, and like any prince, you
        will fall."
        O God, rise up now, judge the earth, for now all the
        nations belong to You!

WEDNESDAY: PSALM 94

הַיּוֹם יוֹם רְבִיעִי בַּשַּׁבָּת שֶׁבּוֹ הָיוּ הַלְוִיִּם אוֹמְרִים
בְּבֵית הַמִּקְדָּשׁ:

1 אֵל־נְקָמוֹת יְהֹוָה אֵל נְקָמוֹת הוֹפִיעַ:

הִנָּשֵׂא שֹׁפֵט הָאָרֶץ הָשֵׁב גְּמוּל עַל־גֵּאִים:

עַד־מָתַי רְשָׁעִים יְהֹוָה עַד־מָתַי רְשָׁעִים יַעֲלֹזוּ:

יַבִּיעוּ יְדַבְּרוּ עָתָק יִתְאַמְּרוּ כָּל־פֹּעֲלֵי אָוֶן:

5 עַמְּךָ יְהֹוָה יְדַכְּאוּ וְנַחֲלָתְךָ יְעַנּוּ:

אַלְמָנָה וְגֵר יַהֲרֹגוּ וִיתוֹמִים יְרַצֵּחוּ:

וַיֹּאמְרוּ לֹא יִרְאֶה־יָּהּ וְלֹא־יָבִין אֱלֹהֵי יַעֲקֹב:

בִּינוּ בֹּעֲרִים בָּעָם וּכְסִילִים מָתַי תַּשְׂכִּילוּ:

הֲנֹטַע אֹזֶן הֲלֹא יִשְׁמָע אִם־יֹצֵר עַיִן הֲלֹא יַבִּיט:

10 הֲיֹסֵר גּוֹיִם הֲלֹא יוֹכִיחַ הַמְלַמֵּד אָדָם דָּעַת:

יְהֹוָה יֹדֵעַ מַחְשְׁבוֹת אָדָם כִּי הֵמָּה הָבֶל:

אַשְׁרֵי הַגֶּבֶר אֲשֶׁר־תְּיַסְּרֶנּוּ יָּהּ וּמִתּוֹרָתְךָ תְלַמְּדֶנּוּ:

לְהַשְׁקִיט לוֹ מִימֵי רָע עַד יִכָּרֶה לָרָשָׁע שָׁחַת:

כִּי לֹא־יִטֹּשׁ יְהֹוָה עַמּוֹ וְנַחֲלָתוֹ לֹא יַעֲזֹב:

WEDNESDAY: PSALM 94

Today is the fourth day of the week, when the Levites sang this
psalm in the Temple:

 1 God of retribution, God who exacts punishment, *Adonai,*
     shine forth!
    Rise up, Judge of all the earth, and give the arrogant what
     they deserve.
    How long, *Adonai,* how long, will the wicked triumph?
    Their arrogance knows no bounds, they boast of their own
     wrongdoing—

 5 they oppress Your people, they mock Your traditions, *Adonai*
    They kill the widow and the foreigner among us, they
     murder orphans,
    they claim that You won't see—that the God of Jacob will
     pay no attention—
    Understand this, you brutes—you fools, see the truth:
    Will the One who formed the ear not hear? Will the Creator
     of the eye not notice?

10 Will the One who rebukes nations, the One who teaches
     awareness,
      fail to punish you?
    Adonai knows our thoughts, knows they are a wisp of wind,
     a mere breath;
    Happy are the ones who feel God's rebuke and learn the
     lesson—
    they can be calm during times of trouble, until evil is
     swallowed up in a pit.
    Adonai will not abandon Israel, those who inherit God's
     teaching:

PSALM 94 (*Continued*)

15 כִּי־עַד־צֶדֶק יָשׁוּב מִשְׁפָּט וְאַחֲרָיו כָּל־יִשְׁרֵי־לֵב:

מִי־יָקוּם לִי עִם־מְרֵעִים מִי־יִתְיַצֵּב לִי עִם־פֹּעֲלֵי אָוֶן:

לוּלֵי יְהוָה עֶזְרָתָה לִּי כִּמְעַט שָׁכְנָה דוּמָה נַפְשִׁי:

אִם־אָמַרְתִּי מָטָה רַגְלִי חַסְדְּךָ יְהוָה יִסְעָדֵנִי:

בְּרֹב שַׂרְעַפַּי בְּקִרְבִּי תַּנְחוּמֶיךָ יְשַׁעַשְׁעוּ נַפְשִׁי:

20 הַיְחָבְרְךָ כִּסֵּא הַוּוֹת יֹצֵר עָמָל עֲלֵי־חֹק:

יָגוֹדּוּ עַל־נֶפֶשׁ צַדִּיק וְדָם נָקִי יַרְשִׁיעוּ:

וַיְהִי יְהוָה לִי לְמִשְׂגָּב וֵאלֹהַי לְצוּר מַחְסִי:

וַיָּשֶׁב עֲלֵיהֶם אֶת־אוֹנָם וּבְרָעָתָם יַצְמִיתֵם יַצְמִיתֵם

יְהוָה אֱלֹהֵינוּ:

PSALM 94 (*Continued*)

15 justice will be restored, and honest hearts will pursue it.
Who will rise up with me against evildoers?
Who will stand with me against the wicked?

If *Adonai* were not my help, my soul would almost be
silenced—
For whenever I feel that I'm stumbling, Your sturdy love,
Adonai,
sets me on my feet.
When my anxieties war within me, You
soothe and console me.

20 You would never lend a hand to leaders whose cruel laws
cause suffering
who band together to persecute the just,
who spill innocent blood.
You are my source of strength, *Adonai,* my God—
You are my refuge—my Rock
who will confront evildoers with their own evil
and utterly destroy them.
Wipe them out.
Adonai our God will wipe them out.

THURSDAY: PSALM 81

הַיּוֹם יוֹם חֲמִישִׁי בַּשַּׁבָּת שֶׁבּוֹ הָיוּ הַלְוִיִּם אוֹמְרִים
בְּבֵית הַמִּקְדָּשׁ:

1 לַמְנַצֵּחַ עַל־הַגִּתִּית לְאָסָף:

הַרְנִינוּ לֵאלֹהִים עוּזֵּנוּ הָרִיעוּ לֵאלֹהֵי יַעֲקֹב:

שְׂאוּ־זִמְרָה וּתְנוּ־תֹף כִּנּוֹר נָעִים עִם־נָבֶל:

תִּקְעוּ בַחֹדֶשׁ שׁוֹפָר בַּכֵּסֶה לְיוֹם חַגֵּנוּ:

5 כִּי חֹק לְיִשְׂרָאֵל הוּא מִשְׁפָּט לֵאלֹהֵי יַעֲקֹב:

עֵדוּת בִּיהוֹסֵף שָׂמוֹ בְּצֵאתוֹ עַל־אֶרֶץ מִצְרָיִם שְׂפַת
לֹא־יָדַעְתִּי אֶשְׁמָע:

הֲסִירוֹתִי מִסֵּבֶל שִׁכְמוֹ כַּפָּיו מִדּוּד תַּעֲבֹרְנָה:

בַּצָּרָה קָרָאתָ וָאֲחַלְּצֶךָּ אֶעֶנְךָ בְּסֵתֶר רַעַם אֶבְחָנְךָ
עַל־מֵי מְרִיבָה סֶלָה:

שְׁמַע עַמִּי וְאָעִידָה בָּךְ יִשְׂרָאֵל אִם־תִּשְׁמַע־לִי:

10 לֹא־יִהְיֶה בְךָ אֵל זָר וְלֹא תִשְׁתַּחֲוֶה לְאֵל נֵכָר:

אָנֹכִי יְהוָה אֱלֹהֶיךָ הַמַּעַלְךָ מֵאֶרֶץ מִצְרָיִם
הַרְחֶב־פִּיךָ וַאֲמַלְאֵהוּ:

וְלֹא־שָׁמַע עַמִּי לְקוֹלִי וְיִשְׂרָאֵל לֹא־אָבָה לִי:

וָאֲשַׁלְּחֵהוּ בִּשְׁרִירוּת לִבָּם יֵלְכוּ בְּמוֹעֲצוֹתֵיהֶם:

לוּ עַמִּי שֹׁמֵעַ לִי יִשְׂרָאֵל בִּדְרָכַי יְהַלֵּכוּ:

15 כִּמְעַט אוֹיְבֵיהֶם אַכְנִיעַ וְעַל־צָרֵיהֶם אָשִׁיב יָדִי:

מְשַׂנְאֵי יְהוָה יְכַחֲשׁוּ־לוֹ וִיהִי עִתָּם לְעוֹלָם:

וַיַּאֲכִילֵהוּ מֵחֵלֶב חִטָּה וּמִצּוּר דְּבַשׁ אַשְׂבִּיעֶךָ:

THURSDAY: PSALM 81

Today is the fifth day of the week, when the Levites sang this
   psalm in the Temple,

1   *For the conductor on the lyre, for Asaph.*
    Sing joyously to God, our source of strength, shout out to
      the God of Jacob!
    Strike up a song, sound the drum, play the sweet harp and
      the lute!
    Blow the shofar for the new moon, the waxing moon
      of our festival day.

5   For that is the law for Israel, the God of Jacob's decree,
      proclaimed at the exodus from Egypt
      (in words we heard but scarcely understood).
    "I freed your suffering shoulders from their burden
      your hands from the weight of bricks—
    You cried out from the straits and I set you free;
      from the hidden source of thunder, I answered you.
    When you thirsted in the desert, I tested you:
    'Hear, My people—I exhort you—Israel, if only you would
      hear Me!

10 *Worship no foreign gods. Never bow down to the god of*
      others:
    I—Adonai—am your God, Who brought you up from the
      land of Egypt:
    Open your mouth wide: I will fill it.'

    "But my people didn't heed My voice. Israel didn't want Me.
    So I let them follow their own willful hearts,
    go their own stubborn way.
    If My people would hear Me, if Israel would walk in My ways,
      I would humble their oppressors—

15 *"I would turn my hand against their foes.*
      Haters of Adonai *would be diminished*
      their time, forever end.
    But Israel I would feed the finest wheat—
    and with honey from the rock, sate them."

FRIDAY: PSALM 93

הַיּוֹם יוֹם שִׁשִּׁי בַּשַּׁבָּת שֶׁבּוֹ הָיוּ הַלְוִיִּם אוֹמְרִים
בְּבֵית הַמִּקְדָּשׁ:

1 יְהֹוָה מָלָךְ גֵּאוּת לָבֵשׁ לָבֵשׁ יְהֹוָה עֹז הִתְאַזָּר אַף־תִּכּוֹן
תֵּבֵל בַּל־תִּמּוֹט:

נָכוֹן כִּסְאֲךָ מֵאָז מֵעוֹלָם אָתָּה:

נָשְׂאוּ נְהָרוֹת יְהֹוָה נָשְׂאוּ נְהָרוֹת קוֹלָם יִשְׂאוּ נְהָרוֹת דָּכְיָם:

מִקֹּלוֹת מַיִם רַבִּים אַדִּירִים מִשְׁבְּרֵי־יָם אַדִּיר בַּמָּרוֹם יְהֹוָה:

5 עֵדֹתֶיךָ נֶאֶמְנוּ מְאֹד לְבֵיתְךָ נָאֲוָה־קֹדֶשׁ יְהֹוָה לְאֹרֶךְ יָמִים:

FRIDAY: PSALM 93

Today is the sixth day of the week, when the Levites sang this
   psalm in the Temple:

1   *Adonai* reigns robed in majesty—*Adonai,* clothed in
      strength—
   making the world unshakable, stable.
   Your throne, *Adonai,* has stood for eons—*You* are from
      forever.
   Though the seas have risen, *Adonai,* the sound of the seas
      has risen, the pounding waves of
      the seas roar
   Stronger than the thundering water, mightier than the
      breakers of the sea,
      is the majesty of *Adonai* on high:

5   For we trust Your Torah, *Adonai,*
   In Your house, the sacred has a home—
   You, *Adonai,* forever.

SHABBAT: PSALM 92

הַיּוֹם שַׁבָּת קֹדֶשׁ שֶׁבּוֹ הָיוּ הַלְוִיִּם אוֹמְרִים בְּבֵית הַמִּקְדָּשׁ:

1   מִזְמוֹר שִׁיר לְיוֹם הַשַּׁבָּת:

טוֹב לְהֹדוֹת לַיהוָה וּלְזַמֵּר לְשִׁמְךָ עֶלְיוֹן:

לְהַגִּיד בַּבֹּקֶר חַסְדֶּךָ וֶאֱמוּנָתְךָ בַּלֵּילוֹת:

עֲלֵי־עָשׂוֹר וַעֲלֵי־נָבֶל עֲלֵי הִגָּיוֹן בְּכִנּוֹר:

5   כִּי שִׂמַּחְתַּנִי יְהוָה בְּפָעֳלֶךָ בְּמַעֲשֵׂי יָדֶיךָ אֲרַנֵּן:

מַה־גָּדְלוּ מַעֲשֶׂיךָ יְהוָה מְאֹד עָמְקוּ מַחְשְׁבֹתֶיךָ:

אִישׁ בַּעַר לֹא יֵדָע וּכְסִיל לֹא־יָבִין אֶת־זֹאת:

בִּפְרֹחַ רְשָׁעִים כְּמוֹ עֵשֶׂב וַיָּצִיצוּ כָּל־פֹּעֲלֵי אָוֶן

לְהִשָּׁמְדָם עֲדֵי־עַד:

וְאַתָּה מָרוֹם לְעֹלָם יְהוָה:

10 כִּי הִנֵּה אֹיְבֶיךָ יְהוָה כִּי־הִנֵּה אֹיְבֶיךָ יֹאבֵדוּ יִתְפָּרְדוּ

כָּל־פֹּעֲלֵי אָוֶן:

וַתָּרֶם כִּרְאֵים קַרְנִי בַּלֹּתִי בְּשֶׁמֶן רַעֲנָן:

וַתַּבֵּט עֵינִי בְּשׁוּרָי בַּקָּמִים עָלַי מְרֵעִים תִּשְׁמַעְנָה אָזְנָי:

צַדִּיק כַּתָּמָר יִפְרָח כְּאֶרֶז בַּלְּבָנוֹן יִשְׂגֶּה:

שְׁתוּלִים בְּבֵית יְהוָה בְּחַצְרוֹת אֱלֹהֵינוּ יַפְרִיחוּ:

15 עוֹד יְנוּבוּן בְּשֵׂיבָה דְּשֵׁנִים וְרַעֲנַנִּים יִהְיוּ:

לְהַגִּיד כִּי־יָשָׁר יְהוָה צוּרִי וְלֹא־עַוְלָתָה בּוֹ:

SHABBAT: PSALM 92

1   *A Sabbath psalm.*
    How good it is to thank *Adonai,* to sing praises
    to our God on high,
    telling of Your kindness in the morning,
    Your loyalty, at night
    with the melodies of the lyre and harp,
    the music of the lute.

5   You have so gladdened me, *Adonai,* by Your works,
        I sing of Your handiwork—creation—
            with joy!

    How great are Your deeds, *Adonai*—Your thoughts
    are so deep—
    The cynical are blind to it— fools don't understand:
    Evil may sprout up like grass—evildoers may flourish,
        but they will be destroyed utterly—
    and You, *Adonai,* will be honored forever.

10 Look, *Adonai,* look, how Your enemies perish,
        how evildoers scatter!
    As if I were a wild ox,
    You raise up my horn in triumph
    You anoint me
    with the freshest oil.
    My eyes see my enemies' downfall,
    my ears hear their defeat.
        But the just are as fertile as a date palm,
            and like a cedar on Mount Lebanon, they grow tall.
        Planted in the House of *Adonai,*
            in the courtyard of our God,
                they blossom

15 They are fresh even in old age,
    fruitful
    luxuriant —
    telling that *Adonai* is true,
        my Rock,
            flawless.

CHAPTER THREE

"You Turned My Grief into Dancing":

Psalm 30 for Every Morning

Perhaps more than any other psalm—with the possible exception of Ps 6 of *Taḥanun*—Psalm 30 is a psalm of transformation. Perhaps it was placed early in our morning service—even before *Pesukei Dezimra*—because it *is* about transformation—and thus can help us make the transition from our sleepy-just-woke-up selves, into "the service of the heart," as our liturgy is called. But the transformation that the psalm depicts is much deeper than that as well.

All tragic drama, according to Aristotle, is about a fall from a high place. If that is true, Ps 30 depicts a tragedy: "You made me strong as a mountain," our psalmist declares—but then "You hid Your face from me, and I was terrified." Life is filled with twists and turns: one day we feel so triumphant, so successful, so strong; the next day, the stock market crashes, the housing market crumbles, we lose our job, we are diagnosed with a serious illness, we lose the campaign we were so confident we would win. In June 1967, Israel went from feeling utterly vulnerable to being ecstatically triumphant; years later, Saddam Hussein rained missiles on Tel Aviv, and in 2006, Hezbollah rockets terrorized Haifa. No aspect of human life, personal or political, promises certainty.

What a powerful psalm this is to turn to during a time of trouble, when we long for relief from suffering. For then, the knowledge of the tumult of life and the inevitable ups-and-downs can serve to remind us that if now we are weeping, with God's help, one day we will be dancing again; if now we are ill, the possibility of a restoration to health is around the corner. One of the most memorable lines from all of the psalms is the one, here, that reminds us that "Weeping may last for a night, but joy comes in the morning." May such mornings come to all of us when we most long for them.

PSALM 30

1   מִזְמוֹר שִׁיר חֲנֻכַּת הַבַּיִת לְדָוִד:

אֲרוֹמִמְךָ יְהוָה כִּי דִלִּיתָנִי וְלֹא־שִׂמַּחְתָּ אֹיְבַי לִי:

יְהוָה אֱלֹהָי שִׁוַּעְתִּי אֵלֶיךָ וַתִּרְפָּאֵנִי:

יְהוָה הֶעֱלִיתָ מִן־שְׁאוֹל נַפְשִׁי חִיִּיתַנִי מִיָּוְרְדִי־ [מִיָּרְדִי] בוֹר:

5   זַמְּרוּ לַיהוָה חֲסִידָיו וְהוֹדוּ לְזֵכֶר קָדְשׁוֹ:

כִּי רֶגַע בְּאַפּוֹ חַיִּים בִּרְצוֹנוֹ בָּעֶרֶב יָלִין בֶּכִי וְלַבֹּקֶר רִנָּה:

וַאֲנִי אָמַרְתִּי בְשַׁלְוִי בַּל־אֶמּוֹט לְעוֹלָם:

יְהוָה בִּרְצוֹנְךָ הֶעֱמַדְתָּה לְהַרְרִי עֹז הִסְתַּרְתָּ פָנֶיךָ

הָיִיתִי נִבְהָל:

אֵלֶיךָ יְהוָה אֶקְרָא וְאֶל־אֲדֹנָי אֶתְחַנָּן:

10 מַה־בֶּצַע בְּדָמִי בְּרִדְתִּי אֶל־שָׁחַת הֲיוֹדְךָ עָפָר הֲיַגִּיד אֲמִתֶּךָ:

שְׁמַע־יְהוָה וְחָנֵּנִי יְהוָה הֱיֵה עֹזֵר לִי:

הָפַכְתָּ מִסְפְּדִי לְמָחוֹל לִי פִּתַּחְתָּ שַׂקִּי וַתְּאַזְּרֵנִי שִׂמְחָה:

לְמַעַן יְזַמֶּרְךָ כָבוֹד וְלֹא יִדֹּם יְהוָה אֱלֹהַי לְעוֹלָם אוֹדֶךָ:

PSALM 30

1 *A song for the dedication of David's Temple.*

I exalt You, *Adonai,* for you have drawn me up
You did not let my enemies rejoice over me.
Adonai my God, I cried to You and You healed me—
Adonai, you raised my soul from the depths
You restored my life when I was nearly in the grave.

5 Sing to *Adonai,* O faithful ones, praise God's holy name,
For God's rage endures but a moment—God's favor is for
  life:
Weeping may last for a night, but joy comes in the morning.

I said, when all went well with me, nothing will ever
  change:
For *Adonai,* You favored me—you made me strong as a
  mountain—
But then You hid Your face from me, and I was terrified.
I cried to You, *Adonai*—I pleaded with You, *Adonai:*
10 "What profit is there in my death, in my descent to the
  grave?
Will dust praise You? Will dust tell of Your truth?
Hear me, *Adonai,* be gracious to me, *Adonai,* help me!"

And then You turned my grief into dancing.
You undid my sackcloth and dressed me in joy—
so that I could sing to You and not be silent—

Adonai my God, I will thank You forever.

CHAPTER FOUR

Falling on Your Face:

Tahanun

At a gathering of rabbinical students last year, one of my colleagues at American Jewish University was asked which part of the morning service meant the most to him.

"I know it sounds odd," he responded, "but I'm drawn most to *Tahanun*."

Many of the students were taken aback. *Tahanun* is a just that part of the service many people famously try to avoid; Hasidim, in fact, omit *Tahanun* on the *yahrzeit*, the anniversary of the death, of every holy rebbe. If there is one part of the morning service in which one really gets to feel like an old-time sinner practicing an old-time religion, *Tahanun*, "Supplications," is it.

The Talmud calls *Tahanun* "Falling on the face" (*nefilat appayim*) (BT Megillah 22a and b), for in ancient times worshippers lay on the floor, arms and legs extended, to pour out their hearts to God. Today we prostrate ourselves so completely only on Yom Kippur; during *Tahanun* we incline to one side, leaning on an elbow. But *Tahanun* remains the time in the service in which we pour out our hearts to God—which is why my colleague so deeply appreciates it.

There were no set prayers for *Tahanun* in ancient days; this was the time to speak to God in your own words. Some of the sages' prayers, though, are recorded in the Talmud—prayers for "love, brotherhood, peace, and companionship" among us

(Rabbi Elazar); prayers that "our hearts not be pained" (Rabbi Ḥiyya), or that we be able to live "a life of goodness, a life of blessing, a life of sustenance, a life of physical health . . . a life free from shame or humiliation" (Rav). Rabbi Mar would pray that God "guard my tongue from evil and my lips from lying" — words that have come to be included in a paragraph after the *Amidah* in many prayer books to this day (BT Brakhot 16b, 17a).

Like so many once unscripted prayer-moments in Judaism, *Taḥanun* has come to have a set liturgy (since the Middle Ages!). Even with the liturgy, though, *Taḥanun* truly gives us a chance to speak to God from the recesses of our own deepest vulnerabilities. That is what Ps 6, traditionally included in *Taḥanun*, does, and what Ps 130, included in *Sim Shalom*, the siddur of the Conservative Movement, also encourages us to do.

PSALM 6

A painful, difficult, psalm — difficult not to grasp intellectually, but to experience, fully, emotionally. Traditional interpretations emphasize that the psalmist is describing the fear and trembling that accompanies being in the throes of physical illness — or for one medieval commentator, the anguish that accompanies having to live in *galut*, "in exile," from the land of Israel. But scarcely *only* illness or *only* exile. Who goes through life free of periods of feeling torn, troubled, overcome by worries, afraid — and so distant from God? Depression can do that; for depression, after all, is not sadness — it is numbness. So can a full-speed-ahead anxiety attack. At the moment anxiety engulfs us, overwhelms us, how trusting are we in the Holy One's abiding, protective care? Or sturdy, compassionate, love?

The first section of the psalm gives such poignant expression to the experience of intense suffering, it is hard to imagine or conceive of relief coming for such an emotional abyss. For me, at least, being in pain — physical, emotional, or spiritual — has often felt like that. The pain is too all encompassing; it feels as if you're closing down.

And then, suddenly, abruptly, relief comes.

What intervened? What brought about the change?

How does change *ever* come about?

What enables us suddenly to cast off grief so that, in the words of the poet W. B. Yeats, all at once and unbidden we suddenly feel as if "we are blessed by everything, and everything we look upon is blessed"? How is it that after sorrow at night, "joy comes in the morning?" What enables someone in the desperate, despairing, throes of an addiction to wake up one day, say the equivalent of "Get away from me, all you evildoers!" to his or her own *yetzer hara*, be able to admit the addiction, and be ready, at last, to get sober, get clean?

The psalmist would express that unfathomable, transcendent—miraculous—moment of transformation by saying "*Adonai* has heard my cry! *Adonai* has heard my plea, *Adonai* will accept my prayer!"

Yes. That explanation convinces me. And you?

PSALM 130

Many of the psalms are rich with a range of words that suggest vast heights: we "exalt" God, God dwells on high, in the heavens, in celestial heights; God is a sovereign over all. At the polar opposite of all those heights is the spiritual place from which Ps 130 springs: *ma'amakkim*, the depths. How powerfully the psalm helps us map our own longing to emerge from those dark and lonely depths—that urgent demand that God listen to us, hear us, so that we need not feel so terribly cut off, so terribly isolated any more. Yes, okay, we've sinned—we've done wrong, the psalmist says on our behalf—but the last thing any of us need is for God to be an obsessive compulsive when it comes to numbering all those sins, all those flaws, each and every possible wrongdoing. And then, in the very center of the psalm, come the words: *You are a forgiving God.* The words are a turning point, for the moment that we do acknowledge that forgiveness is possible, that we are not stuck fast to our past sins like a fly to flypaper, change is possible.

Instead of being trapped in the depths, there is a calm, a willingness to wait with hope and to trust in change.

Moving from the depths of grief to a world of calm, the psalm maps for us how to let go and let God in.

PSALM 6

1   לַמְנַצֵּחַ בִּנְגִינוֹת עַל־הַשְּׁמִינִית מִזְמוֹר לְדָוִד:

יְהֹוָה אַל־בְּאַפְּךָ תוֹכִיחֵנִי וְאַל־בַּחֲמָתְךָ תְיַסְּרֵנִי:

חָנֵּנִי יְהֹוָה כִּי אֻמְלַל אָנִי רְפָאֵנִי יְהֹוָה כִּי נִבְהֲלוּ עֲצָמָי:

וְנַפְשִׁי נִבְהֲלָה מְאֹד וְאַתָּה יְהֹוָה עַד־מָתָי:

5   שׁוּבָה יְהֹוָה חַלְּצָה נַפְשִׁי הוֹשִׁיעֵנִי לְמַעַן חַסְדֶּךָ:

כִּי אֵין בַּמָּוֶת זִכְרֶךָ בִּשְׁאוֹל מִי יוֹדֶה־לָּךְ:

יָגַעְתִּי בְּאַנְחָתִי אַשְׂחֶה בְכָל־לַיְלָה מִטָּתִי בְּדִמְעָתִי

עַרְשִׂי אַמְסֶה:

עָשְׁשָׁה מִכַּעַס עֵינִי עָתְקָה בְּכָל־צוֹרְרָי:

סוּרוּ מִמֶּנִּי כָּל־פֹּעֲלֵי אָוֶן כִּי־שָׁמַע יְהֹוָה קוֹל בִּכְיִי:

10   שָׁמַע יְהֹוָה תְּחִנָּתִי יְהֹוָה תְּפִלָּתִי יִקָּח:

יֵבֹשׁוּ וְיִבָּהֲלוּ מְאֹד כָּל־אֹיְבָי יָשֻׁבוּ יֵבֹשׁוּ רָגַע:

PSALM 6

1   *For the conductor, on the eight-stringed lute, a David psalm.*
    Adonai, do not reprove me in your wrath or punish me in
        Your rage—
    Be gentle with me, *Adonai,* for I am so wretched. Heal me,
        Adonai,
    for my very limbs are trembling with terror, my whole being
        is terrified—
    How long, *Adonai,* how long?

5   Come back to me, *Adonai,* save my life, rescue me
    for the sake of your sturdy love.
    In death, who remembers You? in Sheol, who can praise You?
    I am so weary of moaning. I flood my bed with tears every
        night—
    I drench it with weeping—
    my eyes waste away from grief, they grow dim because of
        my foes.

    Get away from me, all you evildoers! For *Adonai* has heard
        my cry!
10 *Adonai* has heard my plea, *Adonai* will accept my prayer!
    Let those who hate me feel shame—let them relent and—for
        a moment—feel ashamed.

PSALM 130

1 שִׁיר הַמַּעֲלוֹת מִמַּעֲמַקִּים קְרָאתִיךָ יְהֹוָה:

אֲדֹנָי שִׁמְעָה בְקוֹלִי תִּהְיֶינָה אָזְנֶיךָ קַשֻּׁבוֹת לְקוֹל תַּחֲנוּנָי:

אִם־עֲוֹנוֹת תִּשְׁמָר־יָהּ אֲדֹנָי מִי יַעֲמֹד:

כִּי־עִמְּךָ הַסְּלִיחָה לְמַעַן תִּוָּרֵא:

5 קִוִּיתִי יְהֹוָה קִוְּתָה נַפְשִׁי וְלִדְבָרוֹ הוֹחָלְתִּי:

נַפְשִׁי לַאדֹנָי מִשֹּׁמְרִים לַבֹּקֶר שֹׁמְרִים לַבֹּקֶר:

יַחֵל יִשְׂרָאֵל אֶל־יְהֹוָה כִּי־עִם־יְהֹוָה הַחֶסֶד

וְהַרְבֵּה עִמּוֹ פְדוּת:

וְהוּא יִפְדֶּה אֶת־יִשְׂרָאֵל מִכֹּל עֲוֹנֹתָיו:

PSALM 130

1   *A song of ascents.*
Out of the depths I call to You, *Adonai*—
O *Adonai,* hear my voice, let Your ears pay attention
to the sound of my supplications.
If You keep watch for our sins, O God, how can we bear it?
But You are a forgiving God, and for that we feel awe.

Even more than night watchmen, watching for the dawn,
        watch for the dawn,
5   I wait for *Adonai.* My whole being waits. I wait for God's
        word.
O Israel, wait for *Adonai,* for with *Adonai*
is sturdy love and great power to redeem,

And our God *will* redeem Israel
from all of its sins.

CHAPTER FIVE

"*I Bless Your Name Forever and Ever*":

The Daily Hallel

"Rabbi Yose said, 'May my lot in this world and in the world to come be with those who chant the Hallel every day.'" (BT Shabbat 118b)

Most of us associate the Hallel with the jubilant psalms we sing in our congregations on the three pilgrimage festivals—Passover, Shavuot, and Sukkot—along with Hanukkah, Rosh Hodesh, and in our own day, *Yom Ha'atzma'ut*, Israel's Independence Day. Yet, ever since earliest times, those who gathered for morning prayer sought to prepare for their conversation with God by first chanting what ninth-century Rav Sa'adya Ga'on described as "songs and praises to the Holy One." Rav Sa'adya was referring to the six psalms at the very end of the book of Psalms: the "Daily Hallel." On Shabbat morning, the psalms of the Daily Hallel are the climactic end to nine psalms recited in the introductory service, *Pesukei Dezimra*.

So often, in our synagogues, if we actually *do* arrive early enough for *Pesukei Dezimra*, we rush through these psalms, murmuring them full speed ahead, scarcely giving ourselves a chance to experience their soaring, expansive movement and perhaps only barely aware of the glorious journey they are unfolding. But we can go on that journey now. For it *is* glorious. Introduced by lines from earlier psalms affirming our sheer blessedness in being here, now, a Jew among the Jewish people, ready to prepare our soul and spirit for prayer, the psalms spin out from the voice of the single self, praising the greatness and goodness of God, to a call to all of creation to join in that praise; from the lone voice to an orchestra of sound, a celebration of lyres, harps, and flutes, the clang of cymbals and the blasts of the shofar; from the individual ultimately to "everything that breathes." It is as if, as we move from psalm to psalm in the Daily Hallel, we are beckoning the whole universe to come alive and join together in ecstatic praise of the Creator of all. Perhaps, indeed, "praise" is too faint a word to describe such a movement; "vast celebration" is more apt.

To begin that journey, the Daily Hallel opens with language drawn from Pss 86:6 and 144:5, designed to serve as a meditative device, a way of centering ourselves on the sheer blessedness, the happiness, of being in the presence of the *Kadosh Barukh Hu:*

> How blessed are those sitting in your sanctuary, praising You still
> How blessed are the people for whom this is so,
> How blessed, the people whose God is *Adonai!*

PSALM 145 ASHREI

Known as the *Ashrei* for the lines that preface it, Ps 145 may be one of the psalms with which we are most familiar. "I exalt You," begins the psalmist, "every day I bless You"—and indeed, the sages teach us that the psalm *should* be recited every day; three times a day, in fact—in *Pesukei Dezimra;* during *Shaharit,* the morning service, and again during *Minhah,* in the afternoon. But just as our upbeat melodies and cordial familiarity with *Adon Olam* can mask that hymn's spiritual depths, so our frequent— and often very rapid—repetition of the *Ashrei* may lead us to slip right over its riveting message. What, for example, do its opening words, *I exalt You,* actually imply? Has God fallen so low in human history that we must raise God up? Or, from a different perspective, how can any human being exalt God? Isn't God already "exalted"—that is, above and beyond us, beyond our comprehension, whether or not *we* do the exalting?

A teaching of the Hasidic rebbe Mendel of Kotsk casts light on the answer. "Where is God? Mendel of Kotsk was asked. "Wherever you let God in," he responded. For Mendel, to shut oneself off from the possibility of the Divine is the same as saying the Divine is nowhere to be found. Similarly, if it is only our intellects that "let God in," God will appear to us as an intellectual construct; if we open only our hearts, we will worship a God of feeling. At the heart of Mendel of Kotsk's teaching is the assumption that we can experience God only through relationship, only through the gateways to God we ourselves open. ". . . you are My witnesses, declares the Lord, And I am God," says the book of Isaiah (43:12), and the Midrash explains that line as meaning: "If you are my witnesses, I am God; if you are not my witnesses, I am, as it were, not God."

The "Allness" of the Ashrei

In this light, what a witness is the psalmist of the *Ashrei* and what a witness our recitation of the allows us to become! Intricately ordered as an acrostic, moving in Hebrew, from *alef* to *taf*, the psalm overflows with images of abundance—abundant blessing, abundant greatness, abundant compassion, abundant faith. *God is good to* **all**, *close to* **all**; *the guardian of* **all** *who love God; satisfying* **all**, *protecting* **all**, *sovereign of* **all** *worlds*. Along with the vastness of that vision comes, nevertheless, a vivid sense of the individual: **I** will exalt You, **my** God, **my** Sovereign; **I** will bless Your Name forever and ever; May **my** lips *utter praise of God*. If we interpret that "I" as the psalmist, however, we create a barrier between ourselves and the psalm.

For the moment we ourselves speak the words *I will exalt You, my God, my Sovereign*—we are expressing *our* readiness to serve as witnesses as well. Now it is *we* who will be exalting God; *we* who are about to experience what it means for us to feel God as our Sovereign. To say the words "I will bless Your Name forever and ever" is to suggest that the qualities of God we will describe in the lines that follow are also *our* highest ideals, *our* most dearly held values, and ones that reverberate, moreover, beyond the confines of our own life.

Perhaps we could call Ps 145 our "wish list."

What *are* the qualities of the Holy One on that "wish list?" What are the qualities that we laud?

To begin with, in the first stanza, it is the inconceivable *greatness* of God that we focus on: "*Adonai* is great and greatly to be praised, an inconceivable greatness"; a greatness surpassing our ability to intellectually apprehend; beyond analysis, investigation, scrutiny—"inconceivable." Word of the greatness, the "mighty deeds" and "powers" of *Adonai*, is passed on through human history, generation after generation, yet the sense of that greatness is that it is beyond history, beyond even the unbounded time evoked in the opening and the closing lines: *I bless Your Name* **forever** *and* **ever** . . . *I praise Your Name* **forever** *and* **ever** . . . *May all flesh bless the Holy Name* **forever** *and* **ever** . . . **Now** *and* **forever** *shall we bless* Adonai . . . At the very outset, then, the psalm asks us to reach beyond the limitations of time, intellect, and the confines of the individual self to go on a journey into wonder.

There is a paradox, though. For in transcending the self, we are also freeing the self, as the juxtapositions and sheer music of the psalm both suggest. Like the American poet Walt Whitman declaring "I hear America singing," in describing the voice of generations expressing their sense of an awe-inspiring, all-powerful, active God, we are now joining our voice to theirs, as if firmly locating ourselves among the throngs of the human community:

> Each generation acclaims Your mighty deeds to the next, telling of Your powers
> As the majesty—Your glorious majesty—words of your wonders— I speak:
> They speak of Your glorious, astounding, acts—Your greatness, I relate.

The relationship of those lines is reinforced in the original Hebrew, moreover; for the very *sound* of the word for God's "mighty deeds"—*ma'asekha*—is echoed by the sound of the word meaning "I speak" in the next line: *asiḥah*. It is as if one is envisioning a vast chorus of voices praising God and in the very act of doing so, affirming the strength of one's own voice.

Do our intellects argue that such an infinite Presence must be an indifferent force in the universe—that we humans, after all, are less than a speck in time and place? No, the next lines of the psalm tell us: *Adonai* is rather a source of "vast goodness," graciousness, lovingkindness, compassion. Can we truly grant ourselves the permission to experience the spiritual presence in our world of such an unending flow of infinite generosity and love?

The Promise of Infinite Goodness

The psalm suggests that not only is there indeed such love, but also its unbounded energy is *sovereign* of our world, and always has been, and always will be. "Yours is a reign for all time, a reign for every generation," says the psalm. Whatever cruelty we humans have heaped upon one another throughout human history, whatever cruelty we are continuing to heap upon one another today, and whatever violence and injustice reign in our world, there is yet, the psalm insists, a spirit of infinite power and infinite goodness that has been there all along, waiting for us to recognize it fully, to reflect it in our own behavior, a glorious, majestic, principle profoundly worthy of our highest praise. Evil *cannot* triumph, so long as we insist on laying claim to that force of goodness and compassion more powerful than evil—a claim to "the majestic glory" of the "sovereignty" of a God of lovingkindness.

Does this assertion of God's unending goodness pose a dilemma for us? For if we even cursorily review the history of our people, much less human history as a whole, or the terrible destructiveness of nature—the hurricanes, the earthquakes, the tsunamis—how can we insist that God is infinitely good? On the other hand, if we insist, as we do when we speak the words of the psalm, that that goodness is at the very center of our universe, at the center of all life, does that awareness not obligate us to seek to realize it in the world? By going beyond even the human circle—"All *creatures eyes look to You*"—are we not, ourselves, articulating our own recognition that all living beings are God's creatures and thus our compassion too must spread to all that lives? What we are bearing witness to in Ps 145, in other words, is our own highest ideals: what we ourselves yearn for, perhaps what human beings have always yearned for—a world in which the cry of those who suffer is heard, and those who are hungry, are satisfied; a world in which the righteous are rewarded; a world "loving in all deeds"; a world in which we act against evil until it is destroyed. *That* is our God. And that God is closer to us than we may even imagine: for, as the psalmist reminds us,

Adonai *is close to all who call, to all those who truly call.*

PSALM 146

"*May all flesh bless the Holy Name forever and ever, Now and forever shall we bless* Adonai," Ps 145 declared at the end, "*Hallelu-Yah!*" Now comes the first response to that call, Ps 146, with its own shorter, more concentrated, hymn of praise, one whose gaze is more focused on the limitations of human life. The *Ashrei* brimmed over with images of the greatness, glory, and majesty of God, evoking a sense of infinite abundance, utter plenitude. But with Ps 146, it is as if we are grounding ourselves, counterpointing our expression of plenitude with a necessary contraction, a recognition of our transience as humans and our vulnerability. The long lines of the *Ashrei* become the half-lines, the staccato rhythms, of Ps 146. The emphasis on the all-encompassing greatness of God, feeding "*all*," "good to *all*," satisfying "the desires of *all* living creatures," is transformed now into an intense focus on God's concern for the most vulnerable among us: the hungry, the blind, and the widows and orphans.

The contrast with the *Ashrei* becomes clear in the opening lines. Though we embrace the call of the *Ashrei* to praise God—"*Praise* Adonai, *my soul, Halleli!*"—the ecstatic, all-encompassing, visionary enthusiasm of the earlier psalm grows quieter, becomes more modest. "*I exalt you, My God . . . blessing Your Name forever and* ever," said the *Ashrei*. But after all, "forever and ever" is the language of God's realm. We are only human; humans die. The most we can ask of ourselves, then, the most we can promise ourselves is what Ps 146 utters: not praise that will last "forever and ever," but only the hope that "*I will praise* Adonai *all my life, I'll sing to my God* as long as I live."

"As long as I live": to speak those words is a celebration of God, as well as a celebration of the human. But it is also to become aware of the frailty of human life. Who of us does not know a family member or a friend who has died? Someone suffering a serious illness? Those who have suffered the loss of loved ones? The psalm, indeed, implicitly presents us with a profound spiritual challenge: when we fully acknowledge the brevity of life, when we admit that our own lives are merely temporary, can we nevertheless "sing to . . . God," celebrate God, for the time we are given? Can we accept our mortality and yet praise God?

And what would our hymn of praise to God sound like? What would be its melody? What would be its words?

The *Ashrei* offered us mostly a chance to express a majestic vision of the power and the glory of God. The heartbeat of *this* psalm is its celebration of the caring and compassion of the God of Israel, the God our prophets urge us to emulate, the One for whom human life matters. How blessed we are to place our hope in this God! we acknowledge. For the God of Israel is passionately concerned with social justice, with the promise of liberation and freedom. The God who sees the neediness and pain of the world and acts to remedy it. The God of righteousness who will thwart the designs of those who are evil. The God that will not fail us till justice flows like a mighty stream, and the oppressed go free.

To embrace this God is to believe that our world *will* get better; that in the words of Isaiah, "The cry, 'Violence!' shall no more be heard in your land" (60:18). The deep conviction that

> *Adonai* unbinds the bound,
> *Adonai* gives vision to the blind—
> *Adonai* straightens the bent,
> *Adonai* loves the just.
> *Adonai* protects the outsider,
>   helps widows and orphans
>   stand on their feet

is what staves off despair for those trapped in suffering, what serves as a pillar of strength for those who are oppressed. An abiding belief that justice will triumph gives us the determination and courage to fight for that day. We may never be able to complete the task that such a belief sets before us, but as our sages teach us, neither are we free to ignore it.

PSALM 147

After the intensity and power of Ps 146, the tenor abruptly changes. Now, as we move into the very center of the Daily Hallel, our praise of the Almighty and our own spiritual engagement are meant to deepen. "Oh Zion! from generation to generation your God reigns!"—that boldly dramatic public pronouncement with which Ps 146 ended—is transmuted now into the much more gentle opening line of Ps 147, a line intended for our own innermost selves: *"How pleasant and right to make melodies for our God."*

It is a calming line, a way of focusing our attention on the very act in which we're engaged. The line gives us the opportunity to become aware of our own here-and-now experience of *making melodies for our God.* For indeed that *is* what we are doing as we chant the psalms of the Daily Hallel. To savor the pleasantness and feel the rightness of doing *exactly what we are doing now*, to allow ourselves to feel a deep sense of connection to our God, is to open ourselves to an experience of *sheleimut*, of the peace of true wholeness, for many of us a rarely achieved, elusive state. We are coming home to ourselves—an experience, which in turn, deepens the meaning of the next line of the psalm: "Adonai *builds Jerusalem, gathering home the exiles of Israel*."

What does it mean to "build Jerusalem?" Who are the "exiles of Israel?" At first glance, the line seems to cast us back in time to the moment of homecoming and national redemption chronicled in the biblical books of Ezra and Nehemiah, when after long years of exile in Babylon, the Jews were able to return, to rebuild the walls of Jerusalem and restore the Holy Temple. But the grammar of the line interferes with that interpretation, for the line is not in the past tense. The psalmist is not describing *Adonai* as the One who once-upon-a-time-a-long-time-ago rebuilt the city of Jerusalem. Instead, the line suggests that God is *always* engaged in building Jerusalem, whether we think of it literally as the earth-bound city, *Yerushalayim shel mattah*, or as a holy, purely spiritual space, *Yerushalayim shel ma'lah*—as well as on an individual level, the spiritual core, the spiritual home, the place of peace, within each of us. And just as the building of Jerusalem is an ongoing act, so, too, is the experience of the return from exile. For the exiles are not described as *having returned*, as if the return is an act that was performed once and is now complete. Rather, the Hebrew suggests that just as God is *always* building Jerusalem, so, too, the "outcasts" or "exiles" are still and always *in the process of returning*.

For us as individuals, the psalm thus is suggesting that under the aegis of *Adonai*, a return to one's spiritual center is *always* a possibility and that all that keeps us in exile from ourselves—the doubts and uncertainties, the old wounds covered over by a too-thick skin, the fears that may beset us—can *always* be cast off so that we *can* come home. As the eternal Builder of Jerusalem, the Holy One is eternally creating a sanctified spiritual space in which to welcome us home.

Another way to grasp these lines is to feel the potential presence of a sanctified spiritual space—*Yerushalayim*—right here and right now, if we do come home—that is, if we rid ourselves of whatever hinders us from being wholly present *in this very act of prayer and praise.* That may mean letting go of our worries from the day, our discomfort with prayer, our skeptical intellects, our routinized chanting of the psalm—or perhaps of old hurts and old resentments that come between us and a deeply-felt faith. Such letting go is possible, the psalm reminds us. For the One who is eternally building Jerusalem and gathering home the exiles of Israel, is also *"healing the heartbroken, binding their wounds."* In the opening lines of the very center of the Daily Hallel, we are not only being called home, we are being reassured that by coming home, those old heartbreaks, those old wounds, will be healed.

Zooming in on the intensely human, these lines focused on *us* in the act of praying, on God building a sacred space, on hearts in need of healing. Now, though, we suddenly zoom *out,* as if the whole starry expanse of sky is spread before us, witness to the awareness that the God of human healing is also the infinite One who brings order to our universe. Again we find ourselves asking the question we asked in the *Ashrei:* does perceiving God as the One who numbers and names the stars seem to distance God from us? Does this "sky-God" seem unutterably remote? The *Ashrei* went on to describe God's compassion; now, too, lest we find ourselves questioning whether an infinite deity of infinite spaces can possibly relate to inconsequential *us,* the psalm, with a wonderful tenderness, draws us into an integration of the infinite and the intimate. For in the very act of extolling the immensity of God's strength, the immeasurability of God's power—just those qualities that might make us feel so distant from God—the language of the psalm encourages to feel the warmth of our own personal connection. For the first time in the Daily Hallel, the One to whom we are attributing all of these qualities of immeasurability and infinity is referred to, with a sweet intimacy, as "*Adoneinu*" "**our** *Adonai.*"

Throughout the rest of the psalm, this lovely dance of the infinite and intimate continues, becoming like a microcosm of the Daily Hallel as a whole. In the next lines, we describe God at once as architect and engineer of a brilliant ecosystem, controlling the rainfall from the heavens, and at the same time as a tenderly nurturing mother feeding even frail, orphaned, newborn birds. "Not by might and not by power," says the prophet Zekhariah (4:6): making the rain fall, nourishing the cattle, feeding the baby ravens, *Adonai*, says our psalm, is unimpressed by military prowess and sheer brute strength. God yearns for relationship, reciprocity: God is drawn to those who love God, those who in turn trust God's love. I wonder if that's me. If that's us.

"Oh Jerusalem, exalt *Adonai*, sing *Halleluyah* to your God, oh Zion!" come the next lines we say. We who were exiles can be home now. We are Jerusalem. We are Zion. To allow ourselves to feel that now, to feel wholly at one and inside our prayer, is to feel peace "within our borders"; feel fed "with finest wheat." It is truly a moment to savor.

But only a moment. For deep spiritual engagement means never feeling self-satisfied. Just as a rich harvest of crops in the fall is followed by the winter cold, just as victory can be followed by defeat, joyousness can topple into sadness, pleasure into pain, hope into despair; so the image of God lovingly feeding us "choicest wheat" is inevitably followed by wintry images testifying to the potential ferocity of divine power. The same God who nurtures baby birds can scatter snow and frost in the world and hurl hailstones "as if they were breadcrumbs." How well we should know that: who cannot recall the ferocity of earthquakes, tornadoes, hurricanes—or of hardships, setbacks, challenges that we may face in our own lives—to remind ourselves that life is not always "choicest wheat?" That we can feel as if we're bombarded by hailstones? But there is always the promise, says the psalm, that even then there is a moment of miracle, a moment of transformation, the moment we thought would never come: when the frozen world outside or the frozen world within our own breasts "melts," when God "makes the wind blow and the water flow." The hurricane ends; the earth stops quaking; the despair and depression lift; health is restored; the joy of living seems to flow in our veins again. It is as if we are alive again, amazingly ready again to be partners with God in the world.

So alive, indeed, that the final three psalms of the Daily Hallel are like a sunburst of pure, ecstatic, energy. As we pray, it is as if we become conductors of a cosmic orchestra and chorus, calling upon every entity in the universe, every music instrument and every voice—from that of angels in heaven to that of sea creatures in the ocean depths— along with all human beings, young and old, to join in a song of praising God. For Ps 148 reaches out with pulsating energy to the earth and its creatures, to the stars and the highest heavens. Ps 149 reiterates the theme that has been woven into the Daily Hallel from the *Ashrei* on: the disdain of the Holy One for earthly oppressors, along with the love for Israel and for those who are faithful. And, finally, Ps 150 brings the whole series to a jubilant climax by reaching beyond words, and even beyond prayer, to whole-body-praise, the praise of joyous dance and thronging music, of timbrels and lyre, cymbals and flutes, blasts of the shofar—until *every breath of life* is praising the Creator of us all. Perhaps the best response after Ps 150 is a deep breath and a moment of silence in which to feel the power of that praise.

PSALM 145

אַשְׁרֵי יוֹשְׁבֵי בֵיתֶךָ עוֹד יְהַלְלוּךָ סֶּלָה:

אַשְׁרֵי הָעָם שֶׁכָּכָה לּוֹ אַשְׁרֵי הָעָם שֶיְיָ אֱלֹהָיו:

1   תְּהִלָּה לְדָוִד אֲרוֹמִמְךָ אֱלוֹהַי הַמֶּלֶךְ וַאֲבָרְכָה שִׁמְךָ

לְעוֹלָם וָעֶד:

בְּכָל־יוֹם אֲבָרְכֶךָּ וַאֲהַלְלָה שִׁמְךָ לְעוֹלָם וָעֶד:

גָּדוֹל יְהוָה וּמְהֻלָּל מְאֹד וְלִגְדֻלָּתוֹ אֵין חֵקֶר:

דּוֹר לְדוֹר יְשַׁבַּח מַעֲשֶׂיךָ וּגְבוּרֹתֶיךָ יַגִּידוּ:

5   הֲדַר כְּבוֹד הוֹדֶךָ וְדִבְרֵי נִפְלְאוֹתֶיךָ אָשִׂיחָה:

וֶעֱזוּז נוֹרְאֹתֶיךָ יֹאמֵרוּ וּגְדוּלָּתֶיךָ [וּגְדוּלָּתְךָ] אֲסַפְּרֶנָּה:

זֵכֶר רַב־טוּבְךָ יַבִּיעוּ וְצִדְקָתְךָ יְרַנֵּנוּ:

חַנּוּן וְרַחוּם יְהוָה אֶרֶךְ אַפַּיִם וּגְדָל־חָסֶד:

טוֹב־יְהוָה לַכֹּל וְרַחֲמָיו עַל־כָּל־מַעֲשָׂיו:

10   יוֹדוּךָ יְהוָה כָּל־מַעֲשֶׂיךָ וַחֲסִידֶיךָ יְבָרְכוּכָה:

כְּבוֹד מַלְכוּתְךָ יֹאמֵרוּ וּגְבוּרָתְךָ יְדַבֵּרוּ:

לְהוֹדִיעַ לִבְנֵי הָאָדָם גְּבוּרֹתָיו וּכְבוֹד הֲדַר מַלְכוּתוֹ:

מַלְכוּתְךָ מַלְכוּת כָּל־עֹלָמִים וּמֶמְשֶׁלְתְּךָ בְּכָל־דּוֹר וָדוֹר:

סוֹמֵךְ יְהוָה לְכָל־הַנֹּפְלִים וְזוֹקֵף לְכָל־הַכְּפוּפִים:

PSALM 145

1   *David's Song of Praise.*
> I exalt You, My God, my Sovereign, I bless Your Name
>   forever and ever
> Each and every day I bless You, I praise Your Name forever
>   and ever

> *Adonai* is great and greatly to be praised, an inconceivable
>   greatness,
> Each generation praising Your mighty deeds to the next,
>   telling of Your powers

5   As the majesty—Your glorious majesty—words of Your
>   wonders—I speak:
> They speak of Your glorious, astounding, acts—Your
>   greatness, I relate:

> Endlessly celebrating Your vast goodness, singing
>   with joy of Your tender acts
> *"Adonai is gracious and compassionate, slow to anger,*
>   *abounding in lovingkindness."*
> Good to all is *Adonai,* compassionate in all deeds.

10   All Your works praise You, *Adonai,* and all those faithful to
>   You bless You:

> They tell of the glorious splendor of Your sovereignty; they
>   speak of Your power
> They tell all humanity of Your mighty acts, the majestic glory
>   of the sovereignty of God.

> Yours is a reign for all time, a reign for every generation.

> *Adonai* is support for all who fall, the raiser of all the
>   subjugated.

PSALM 145 (*Continued*)

15 עֵינֵי כֹל אֵלֶיךָ יְשַׂבֵּרוּ וְאַתָּה נוֹתֵן־לָהֶם אֶת־אָכְלָם בְּעִתּוֹ:

פוֹתֵחַ אֶת־יָדֶךָ וּמַשְׂבִּיעַ לְכָל־חַי רָצוֹן:

צַדִּיק יְהֹוָה בְּכָל־דְּרָכָיו וְחָסִיד בְּכָל־מַעֲשָׂיו:

קָרוֹב יְהֹוָה לְכָל־קֹרְאָיו לְכֹל אֲשֶׁר יִקְרָאֻהוּ בֶאֱמֶת:

רְצוֹן־יְרֵאָיו יַעֲשֶׂה וְאֶת־שַׁוְעָתָם יִשְׁמַע וְיוֹשִׁיעֵם:

20 שׁוֹמֵר יְהֹוָה אֶת־כָּל־אֹהֲבָיו וְאֵת כָּל־הָרְשָׁעִים יַשְׁמִיד:

תְּהִלַּת יְהֹוָה יְדַבֶּר־פִּי וִיבָרֵךְ כָּל־בָּשָׂר שֵׁם קָדְשׁוֹ

לְעוֹלָם וָעֶד:

PSALM 145 (*Continued*)

15   All creatures' eyes look to You and You provide
       food in its season:
  opening Your hand, satisfying the desire of all living
       creatures.
  Righteous is *Adonai* in all ways, loving in all deeds,
  Adonai is close to all who call, to all those who truly call,
  Fulfilling the desire of those who hold You in awe, hearing
       their cry, saving them,

20   For *Adonai* protects those who love the Eternal and destroys
       the evil-doers.

    Out of my mouth pours praise of Adonai—*may all flesh*
        bless the Holy Name forever and ever
    Now and forever shall we bless Adonai, *Hallelu-Yah!*

PSALM 146

1 הַלְלוּיָהּ הַלְלִי נַפְשִׁי אֶת־יְהֹוָה:

אֲהַלְלָה יְהֹוָה בְּחַיָּי אֲזַמְּרָה לֵאלֹהַי בְּעוֹדִי:

אַל־תִּבְטְחוּ בִנְדִיבִים בְּבֶן־אָדָם שֶׁאֵין לוֹ תְשׁוּעָה:

תֵּצֵא רוּחוֹ יָשֻׁב לְאַדְמָתוֹ בַּיּוֹם הַהוּא אָבְדוּ עֶשְׁתֹּנֹתָיו:

5 אַשְׁרֵי שֶׁאֵל יַעֲקֹב בְּעֶזְרוֹ שִׂבְרוֹ עַל־יְהֹוָה אֱלֹהָיו:

עֹשֶׂה שָׁמַיִם וָאָרֶץ אֶת־הַיָּם וְאֶת־כָּל־אֲשֶׁר־בָּם הַשֹּׁמֵר

אֱמֶת לְעוֹלָם:

עֹשֶׂה מִשְׁפָּט לַעֲשׁוּקִים נֹתֵן לֶחֶם לָרְעֵבִים

יְהֹוָה מַתִּיר אֲסוּרִים:

יְהֹוָה פֹּקֵחַ עִוְרִים יְהֹוָה זֹקֵף כְּפוּפִים יְהֹוָה אֹהֵב צַדִּיקִים:

יְהֹוָה שֹׁמֵר אֶת־גֵּרִים יָתוֹם וְאַלְמָנָה יְעוֹדֵד

וְדֶרֶךְ רְשָׁעִים יְעַוֵּת:

10 יִמְלֹךְ יְהֹוָה לְעוֹלָם אֱלֹהַיִךְ צִיּוֹן לְדֹר וָדֹר הַלְלוּיָהּ:

PSALM 146

1 Praise *Adonai,* my soul! *Halleli*—
I will praise *Adonai* all my life, I'll sing to my God as long as
I live.

Put no trust in people of power—flesh and blood can offer
no deliverance—
They breathe their last, return to earth,
and on that day, their plans perish.

5 But blessed are those whom the God of Jacob helps—
those who hope in their God *Adonai,*
Maker of heaven, earth and sea, of all they contain,
Guardian of truth forever,
meting out justice for the oppressed, food to the hungry.
Adonai unbinds the bound,
Adonai gives vision to the blind—
Adonai straightens the bent,
Adonai loves the just.
Adonai protects the outsider, helping widows and orphans
stand on their feet,
and the path of the wicked, thwarts.

10 *Adonai* reigns forever and ever; oh Zion, from generation to
generation your God reigns! *Hallelu-Yah!*

PSALM 147

1 הַלְלוּיָהּ כִּי־טוֹב זַמְּרָה אֱלֹהֵינוּ כִּי־נָעִים נָאוָה תְהִלָּה:

בּוֹנֵה יְרוּשָׁלַם יְהוָה נִדְחֵי יִשְׂרָאֵל יְכַנֵּס:

הָרֹפֵא לִשְׁבוּרֵי לֵב וּמְחַבֵּשׁ לְעַצְּבוֹתָם:

מוֹנֶה מִסְפָּר לַכּוֹכָבִים לְכֻלָּם שֵׁמוֹת יִקְרָא:

5 גָּדוֹל אֲדוֹנֵינוּ וְרַב־כֹּחַ לִתְבוּנָתוֹ אֵין מִסְפָּר:

מְעוֹדֵד עֲנָוִים יְהוָה מַשְׁפִּיל רְשָׁעִים עֲדֵי־אָרֶץ:

עֱנוּ לַיהוָה בְּתוֹדָה זַמְּרוּ לֵאלֹהֵינוּ בְכִנּוֹר:

הַמְכַסֶּה שָׁמַיִם בְּעָבִים הַמֵּכִין לָאָרֶץ מָטָר הַמַּצְמִיחַ
הָרִים חָצִיר:

נוֹתֵן לִבְהֵמָה לַחְמָהּ לִבְנֵי עֹרֵב אֲשֶׁר יִקְרָאוּ:

10 לֹא בִגְבוּרַת הַסּוּס יֶחְפָּץ לֹא־בְשׁוֹקֵי הָאִישׁ יִרְצֶה:

רוֹצֶה יְהוָה אֶת־יְרֵאָיו אֶת־הַמְיַחֲלִים לְחַסְדּוֹ:

שַׁבְּחִי יְרוּשָׁלַיִם אֶת־יְהוָה הַלְלִי אֱלֹהַיִךְ צִיּוֹן:

כִּי־חִזַּק בְּרִיחֵי שְׁעָרָיִךְ בֵּרַךְ בָּנַיִךְ בְּקִרְבֵּךְ:

הַשָּׂם גְּבוּלֵךְ שָׁלוֹם חֵלֶב חִטִּים יַשְׂבִּיעֵךְ:

PSALM 147

1 *Hallelu-Yah!*
   How pleasant and right it is to make melodies for our God,
      how sweet the beauty of a song of praise!

   Adonai builds Jerusalem,
      gathering home the exiles of Israel,
   healing the heartbroken,
   binding their wounds—

   numbering the stars, calling them each by name.

5 How great our *Adonai,* how immensely strong, how beyond
      number or measure is Divine wisdom.
   Adonai stands the oppressed on their feet
   casting the wicked
   to the very ground.

   Sing to *Adonai* with gratitude! Make melodies to our God
      with the lyre!
   For God veils the sky with clouds
   readying the earth for rain,
   so grass will grow on the hills, nourishing
   the grazing cattle
      and even newborn ravens who cry out.

10 God takes no delight in a stallion's strength; finds no
      pleasure in the might of a warrior—
   Adonai takes pleasure in those who feel awe,
   in those who depend on God's sturdy love.

   Oh, Jerusalem, exalt *Adonai,* sing *Halleluyah* to your God,
      oh Zion—
   For God has strengthened your city's gates and blessed the
      children within you,
   God has brought peace to your borders and filled you with
      the finest wheat.

PSALM 147 (*Continued*)

15 הַשֹּׁלֵחַ אִמְרָתוֹ אָרֶץ עַד־מְהֵרָה יָרוּץ דְּבָרוֹ:

הַנֹּתֵן שֶׁלֶג כַּצָּמֶר כְּפוֹר כָּאֵפֶר יְפַזֵּר:

מַשְׁלִיךְ קַרְחוֹ כְפִתִּים לִפְנֵי קָרָתוֹ מִי יַעֲמֹד:

יִשְׁלַח דְּבָרוֹ וְיַמְסֵם יַשֵּׁב רוּחוֹ יִזְּלוּ־מָיִם:

מַגִּיד דְּבָרָיו לְיַעֲקֹב חֻקָּיו וּמִשְׁפָּטָיו לְיִשְׂרָאֵל:

20 לֹא עָשָׂה כֵן לְכָל־גּוֹי וּמִשְׁפָּטִים בַּל־יְדָעוּם הַלְלוּיָהּ:

PSALM 147 (*Continued*)

15 God sends a command to earth—how swiftly God's word
      runs—
    Scattering snow as if it were fleece, scattering frost as if it
      were ash
        hurling hailstones like crumbs of bread—who can
          withstand
        the cold of God?
    But with a word God melts it all,
    making the wind blow and water flow.

    God spoke the Word to Jacob;
      and the Torah, only to Israel.
20 God has not dealt so with other nations;
    God's Torah was unknown to them.
        Hallelu-Yah!

PSALM 148

1 הַלְלוּיָהּ הַלְלוּ אֶת־יְהֹוָה מִן־הַשָּׁמַיִם הַלְלוּהוּ בַּמְּרוֹמִים׃

הַלְלוּהוּ כָל־מַלְאָכָיו הַלְלוּהוּ כָּל־צְבָאָו צְבָאָיו׃

הַלְלוּהוּ שֶׁמֶשׁ וְיָרֵחַ הַלְלוּהוּ כָּל־כּוֹכְבֵי אוֹר׃

הַלְלוּהוּ שְׁמֵי הַשָּׁמָיִם וְהַמַּיִם אֲשֶׁר מֵעַל הַשָּׁמָיִם׃

5 יְהַלְלוּ אֶת־שֵׁם יְהֹוָה כִּי הוּא צִוָּה וְנִבְרָאוּ׃

וַיַּעֲמִידֵם לָעַד לְעוֹלָם חָק־נָתַן וְלֹא יַעֲבוֹר׃

הַלְלוּ אֶת־יְהֹוָה מִן־הָאָרֶץ תַּנִּינִים וְכָל־תְּהֹמוֹת׃

אֵשׁ וּבָרָד שֶׁלֶג וְקִיטוֹר רוּחַ סְעָרָה עֹשָׂה דְבָרוֹ׃

הֶהָרִים וְכָל־גְּבָעוֹת עֵץ פְּרִי וְכָל־אֲרָזִים׃

10 הַחַיָּה וְכָל־בְּהֵמָה רֶמֶשׂ וְצִפּוֹר כָּנָף׃

מַלְכֵי־אֶרֶץ וְכָל־לְאֻמִּים שָׂרִים וְכָל־שֹׁפְטֵי אָרֶץ׃

בַּחוּרִים וְגַם־בְּתוּלוֹת זְקֵנִים עִם־נְעָרִים׃

יְהַלְלוּ אֶת־שֵׁם יְהֹוָה כִּי־נִשְׂגָּב שְׁמוֹ לְבַדּוֹ

הוֹדוֹ עַל־אֶרֶץ וְשָׁמָיִם׃

וַיָּרֶם קֶרֶן לְעַמּוֹ תְּהִלָּה לְכָל־חֲסִידָיו לִבְנֵי יִשְׂרָאֵל

עַם־קְרֹבוֹ הַלְלוּיָהּ׃

PSALM 148

1 *Hallelu-Yah!*
   Praise *Adonai* from the heavens! Praise *Adonai* in the skies!
   Praise *Adonai,* angels of heaven—praise God, all angelic
      troops!
   Praise God, oh sun and moon! Praise God, all resplendent
      stars!
   Praise God, highest heavens and waters beyond the heavens!

5 Let them praise the name of *Adonai* who commanded their
      creation,
   Establishing them forever and ever, setting them bounds
      never to be crossed.

   Praise *Adonai* from the earth, creatures of the sea and all
      darkest depths!
   Fire and hail, snow and smoke, storming wind, doing the
      All-Powerful's bidding!
   The mountains and all hills, the fruit trees and all cedars—
10 Wild animals and all the tamed, creeping creatures and
      birds who fly—
   Monarchs of the earth and all peoples, leaders and all who
      rule
   Young men and young women, the aged along with the
      youth:
   Let us praise the name *Adonai,* for that name alone is
      exalted,
   The splendor of God is over all heaven and earth.

   The Almighty exalts the people of God, praising all the faithful,
      praising Israel, the people close to God. *Hallelu-Yah!*

PSALM 149

1   הַלְלוּיָהּ שִׁירוּ לַיהוָה שִׁיר חָדָשׁ תְּהִלָּתוֹ בִּקְהַל חֲסִידִים:

יִשְׂמַח יִשְׂרָאֵל בְּעֹשָׂיו בְּנֵי־צִיּוֹן יָגִילוּ בְמַלְכָּם:

יְהַלְלוּ שְׁמוֹ בְמָחוֹל בְּתֹף וְכִנּוֹר יְזַמְּרוּ־לוֹ:

כִּי־רוֹצֶה יְהוָה בְּעַמּוֹ יְפָאֵר עֲנָוִים בִּישׁוּעָה:

5   יַעְלְזוּ חֲסִידִים בְּכָבוֹד יְרַנְּנוּ עַל־מִשְׁכְּבוֹתָם:

רוֹמְמוֹת אֵל בִּגְרוֹנָם וְחֶרֶב פִּיפִיּוֹת בְּיָדָם:

לַעֲשׂוֹת נְקָמָה בַּגּוֹיִם תּוֹכֵחֹת בַּל־אֻמִּים:

לֶאְסֹר מַלְכֵיהֶם בְּזִקִּים וְנִכְבְּדֵיהֶם בְּכַבְלֵי בַרְזֶל:

לַעֲשׂוֹת בָּהֶם מִשְׁפָּט כָּתוּב הָדָר הוּא לְכָל־חֲסִידָיו הַלְלוּיָהּ:

PSALM 149

1 *Hallelu-Yah!*

Sing a new song to *Adonai,* praise *Adonai* among the faithful

Let Israel rejoice in their Maker, let the people of Zion celebrate their Sovereign!

Let them dance in praise of the Name, making music for God with timbrel and lyre,

For *Adonai* delights in this people and with victory crowns the meek.

5 Let the faithful rejoice in glory, let them shout in joy at their feast—

high praises of God in their throat—but a double-edged sword in their hand:

to demand recompense from the nations and to chastise the peoples of the world

to shackle the hands of their kings and lock in fetters their nobles' feet,

to impose the verdict decreed for them and bring glory to God's faithful—

Hallelu-Yah!

PSALM 150

1   הַלְלוּיָהּ הַלְלוּ־אֵל בְּקָדְשׁוֹ הַלְלוּהוּ בִּרְקִיעַ עֻזּוֹ:

הַלְלוּהוּ בִגְבוּרֹתָיו הַלְלוּהוּ כְּרֹב גֻּדְלוֹ:

הַלְלוּהוּ בְּתֵקַע שׁוֹפָר הַלְלוּהוּ בְּנֵבֶל וְכִנּוֹר:

הַלְלוּהוּ בְתֹף וּמָחוֹל הַלְלוּהוּ בְּמִנִּים וְעוּגָב:

5   הַלְלוּהוּ בְצִלְצְלֵי־שָׁמַע הַלְלוּהוּ בְּצִלְצְלֵי תְרוּעָה:

כֹּל הַנְּשָׁמָה תְּהַלֵּל יָהּ הַלְלוּיָהּ:

PSALM 150

1 *Hallelu-Yah!*

   Hallelu-El in God's sanctuary! *Halleluhu* in the heavens of
     God's power!

   Halleluhu for mighty deeds! *Halleluhu* for abundant
     greatness!

   Praise God with shofar blasts! Praise God with harps and
     lyres!

   Praise God with timbrels and dance! Praise God with strings
     and flutes!

5 Praise God with clanging cymbals—Praise God with the
     cymbals' clash!

   Let every breath of life praise God, *Hallelu-Yah!*

CHAPTER SIX

Ecstatic Salvation:

The Psalms of the Festival Hallel

God liberates Israel from slavery in Egypt and all nature is affected: the sea flees to allow the people of Israel to escape from Pharaoh's army, the Jordan River rolls back so that they can enter into Canaan; trembling at the sight of this newly born nation, the surrounding mountains skip like rams, and the whole earth whirls!

A childless woman becomes a mother.

The poor are seated with the rich.

Once gripped by anguish and the threat of imminent death, a person wakes up to walk again with *Adonai* "in the land of the living." Saved from enemies who once "swarmed like bees," a grateful speaker exclaims, "I will not die but live / so I can recount the deeds of *Adonai!*"

> Return, O my soul, to a sense of ease, for *Adonai* has dealt
> bountifully with you! (Ps 116)

The word "salvation" doesn't feel very Jewish. In Western culture, under the influence of Christian theology, the word has evolved from its original range of meanings to mean "saved from sin." Yet *yeshu'ah*, the Hebrew word for "salvation," does not mean "saved from sin," nor can it really be reduced to mean only "rescue." When you're rescued, you're returned to safety—thrown a life raft, grabbed from under a burning car, handed a cell phone. But to be *saved* in a spiritual sense is more than being rescued. To be "saved" is to be rescued *and* transformed.

And it is both rescue and transformation—*salvation*—that the Hallel, joyously and robustly sung on the Jewish festivals (and in part on Rosh Hodesh), celebrates. Indeed, what these ancient psalms most remarkably express is the ecstasy of salvation, both personal and collective: the salvation of the people and nation of Israel, and the salvation of every individual who has suffered poverty, serious illness, infertility, crippling fear, anguish, despair. The very imagery of the Hallel transports us back to the Temple in Jerusalem; if you listen closely, you can almost hear the pilgrims calling for the opening of the gates and then pouring into at the Temple courtyard to the sound of the Levites' cymbals, drums, trumpets and lyres, and the ancient call-and-response:

> Let Israel now say, "God's kindness is forever!"
> Let the House of Aaron now say, "God's kindness is forever!"
> Let all those who worship *Adonai* now say, "God's kindness is forever!" (Ps 118)[10]

As public and as national a celebration as the Festival Hallel is, though, it also gazes out both at the whole human world and at the individual soul. It calls upon all humanity, as well as the whole of Israel and each of us, and encourages, along with its calls for celebration and praise, a deeply private, deeply individualized, personal contemplation.

It opens with a universal call: Ps 113 is meant for "*All* those who worship *Adonai*," not Israel alone. And why not universal, for God is not Israel's private possession. God, the psalm tells us, is "above

---

[10]See, for example, Reuven Hammer, *Or Hadash: A Commentary on Siddur Sim Shalom* (New York: Rabbinical Assembly, 2003), p. 134.

all nations," above all national divisions and is both immanent and transcendent—"dwelling in celestial heights" but also altering human life out of a commitment to the helpless and needy:

> Stooping down to look into heaven and earth:
> raising the poor from the dust—the destitute, from a heap of ashes. (Ps 113)

Only then does the Hallel zoom in on the experience of Israel, rendered in Ps 114 in tones at once dramatic, miraculous, world-changing, and spiritually alive. As Israel emerges like a baby from the womb, it becomes the special "domain" and "sanctuary" of the Holy One, interrupting the course of nature. God comes into history as a transformative force, whirling the earth around and (with no mention of Moses' rod!) turning "rocks into pools of water." Ps 115 is like a pause, dismissing the gods that human beings fashion with their own hands, and calling for a radically different kind of reciprocity between humans and their God, the reciprocity of mutual blessing:

> *Adonai* has been mindful of us and will bless us . . .
> May our God bless all believers, young or old . . .
> Blessed are you by *Adonai*, Maker of heaven and earth . . .
> . . . we will bless *Adonai* now and forevermore. (Ps 115)

And then, from the universal to the national, the Festival Hallel transitions to the individual. Movingly, in Ps 116 the medieval commentator Rashi hears the voice of David, who, after years of being relentlessly pursued by a maddened King Saul, is faced with Saul's death, the death of his beloved friend Jonathan, and at last, his own coronation as king:

> For, my soul, you were saved from death—and my eyes from
> tears,
>   my feet from stumbling:
> I will walk with *Adonai* in the land of the living.

Even when I said "I am in great pain," I still had faith —
even when I so rashly said
life is a mere illusion!
Now what can I give back to *Adonai*
for all *Adonai's* bounty
to me?

Yet, with all the wrenching drama in David's life, the radical, unexpected transformation from near-death to renewed life, from the depths of despair to what is at once humbled but also ecstatic gratitude, is not unique to him. Rather, that kind of transformation has been and is shared by so many of us, an experience in which what seemed the logical, predictable, even *inevitable* outcome is defied. Somehow, unaccountably, *miracle* intervened. The sea parted, and you made it across. Water sprang out from the desert rock. Whether or not we have ever suffered as drastically as the psalmist, truly, line after line, Ps 116 invites deeply personal contemplation. ". . . what can I give back to *Adonai* for all *Adonai's* bounty to me?" the psalmist asks. Focused on what we "need" that we do not have, we may not often (enough) feel the bounty that already exists in our lives. But, as the book of Deuteronomy reminds us, we make a grave error to claim "My power and the might of my own hand have won this wealth for me" (8:17). For how can we take for granted as a natural right, or even as an earned right, the ineffable bounty that comes from having people to love, plenty to eat, a house to live in, good health, good work, and a life free of the ravages of suffering that still plague most human beings on our planet? Who among us is to say that *we* deserve what we have been given, but another — another who is kind, and good, and thoughtful, but also ravaged by disease, or desperately poor — does not? Our Festival Hallel, even as it celebrates the triumph of Israel and the goodness of God, urges us to count our blessings . . . and to seek to live a life worthy of those blessings. Then we will truly feel that "the kindness of *Adonai* overwhelms us!" (Ps 117). *Hallelu-Yah!*

PSALM 113

הַלְלוּיָהּ הַלְלוּ עַבְדֵי יְהֹוָה הַלְלוּ אֶת־שֵׁם יְהֹוָה: 1

יְהִי שֵׁם יְהֹוָה מְבֹרָךְ מֵעַתָּה וְעַד־עוֹלָם:

מִמִּזְרַח־שֶׁמֶשׁ עַד־מְבוֹאוֹ מְהֻלָּל שֵׁם יְהֹוָה:

רָם עַל־כָּל־גּוֹיִם יְהֹוָה עַל הַשָּׁמַיִם כְּבוֹדוֹ:

מִי כַּיהֹוָה אֱלֹהֵינוּ הַמַּגְבִּיהִי לָשָׁבֶת: 5

הַמַּשְׁפִּילִי לִרְאוֹת בַּשָּׁמַיִם וּבָאָרֶץ:

מְקִימִי מֵעָפָר דָּל מֵאַשְׁפֹּת יָרִים אֶבְיוֹן:

לְהוֹשִׁיבִי עִם־נְדִיבִים עִם נְדִיבֵי עַמּוֹ:

מוֹשִׁיבִי עֲקֶרֶת הַבַּיִת אֵם־הַבָּנִים שְׂמֵחָה הַלְלוּיָהּ:

PSALM 113

1 *Hallelu-Yah!*
All those who worship *Adonai,* praise *Adonai,* praise the
name *Adonai!*
May the name *Adonai* be blessed from this moment on,
forever!
From sunrise to sunset, east to west, praised be the name
Adonai!
Above all nations is *Adonai,* whose glory
is above even the heavens—

5 Who is like *Adonai* our God, dwelling in celestial heights,
stooping down to look into heaven and earth:
raising the poor from the dust,
and the destitute from a heap of ashes—
setting them next to the elite—the elite of their own
people—
and settling a childless woman in her own home,
to become the joyous mother of children?

PSALM 114

1   בְּצֵאת יִשְׂרָאֵל מִמִּצְרָיִם בֵּית יַעֲקֹב מֵעַם לֹעֵז:

הָיְתָה יְהוּדָה לְקָדְשׁוֹ יִשְׂרָאֵל מַמְשְׁלוֹתָיו:

הַיָּם רָאָה וַיָּנֹס הַיַּרְדֵּן יִסֹּב לְאָחוֹר:

הֶהָרִים רָקְדוּ כְאֵילִים גְּבָעוֹת כִּבְנֵי־צֹאן:

5   מַה־לְּךָ הַיָּם כִּי תָנוּס הַיַּרְדֵּן תִּסֹּב לְאָחוֹר:

הֶהָרִים תִּרְקְדוּ כְאֵילִים גְּבָעוֹת כִּבְנֵי־צֹאן:

מִלִּפְנֵי אָדוֹן חוּלִי אָרֶץ מִלִּפְנֵי אֱלוֹהַּ יַעֲקֹב:

הַהֹפְכִי הַצּוּר אֲגַם־מָיִם חַלָּמִישׁ לְמַעְיְנוֹ־מָיִם:

PSALM 114

1 As Israel came out of Egypt,
   the house of Jacob from a foreign land
   Judah became God's sanctuary and Israel, God's domain.
   The sea saw and fled—the Jordan turned back—
   The mountains skipped like rams— and the hills
   like a herd of sheep!

5 O sea, why did you flee? O Jordan, why retreat?
   why did you mountains skip like rams,
   and you hills like sheep?
   At the presence of God
      —even earth whirled around—
   at the presence of the God of Jacob
      Who turns rocks into pools of water and flintstones
   into springs.

PSALM 115

1   לֹא לָנוּ יְהוָה לֹא לָנוּ כִּי־לְשִׁמְךָ תֵּן כָּבוֹד עַל־חַסְדְּךָ
עַל־אֲמִתֶּךָ:

לָמָּה יֹאמְרוּ הַגּוֹיִם אַיֵּה־נָא אֱלֹהֵיהֶם:

וֵאלֹהֵינוּ בַשָּׁמָיִם כֹּל אֲשֶׁר־חָפֵץ עָשָׂה:

עֲצַבֵּיהֶם כֶּסֶף וְזָהָב מַעֲשֵׂה יְדֵי אָדָם:

5   פֶּה־לָהֶם וְלֹא יְדַבֵּרוּ עֵינַיִם לָהֶם וְלֹא יִרְאוּ:

אָזְנַיִם לָהֶם וְלֹא יִשְׁמָעוּ אַף לָהֶם וְלֹא יְרִיחוּן:

יְדֵיהֶם וְלֹא יְמִישׁוּן רַגְלֵיהֶם וְלֹא יְהַלֵּכוּ לֹא־יֶהְגּוּ בִּגְרוֹנָם:

כְּמוֹהֶם יִהְיוּ עֹשֵׂיהֶם כֹּל אֲשֶׁר־בֹּטֵחַ בָּהֶם:

יִשְׂרָאֵל בְּטַח בַּיהוָה עֶזְרָם וּמָגִנָּם הוּא:

10   בֵּית אַהֲרֹן בִּטְחוּ בַיהוָה עֶזְרָם וּמָגִנָּם הוּא:

יִרְאֵי יְהוָה בִּטְחוּ בַיהוָה עֶזְרָם וּמָגִנָּם הוּא:

יְהוָה זְכָרָנוּ יְבָרֵךְ יְבָרֵךְ אֶת־בֵּית יִשְׂרָאֵל יְבָרֵךְ
אֶת־בֵּית אַהֲרֹן:

יְבָרֵךְ יִרְאֵי יְהוָה הַקְּטַנִּים עִם־הַגְּדֹלִים:

יֹסֵף יְהוָה עֲלֵיכֶם עֲלֵיכֶם וְעַל־בְּנֵיכֶם:

15   בְּרוּכִים אַתֶּם לַיהוָה עֹשֵׂה שָׁמַיִם וָאָרֶץ:

הַשָּׁמַיִם שָׁמַיִם לַיהוָה וְהָאָרֶץ נָתַן לִבְנֵי־אָדָם:

לֹא הַמֵּתִים יְהַלְלוּ־יָהּ וְלֹא כָּל־יֹרְדֵי דוּמָה:

וַאֲנַחְנוּ נְבָרֵךְ יָהּ מֵעַתָּה וְעַד־עוֹלָם הַלְלוּיָהּ:

PSALM 115

1 Not to us, *Adonai,* not to us, but to Your own name give glory
because of Your kindness and Your sturdy truth
Why should other nations say, "Where is their god?"
while You dwell in heaven doing as You will:
They worship gold and silver gods, made with their own hands:

5 Their gods have mouths that can't speak; they have eyes that
can't see
They have ears that can't hear—a nose they have that can't
smell.
Their hands don't feel, their feet don't walk,
no sound comes out of their throat:
Their makers will become just like them, along with all who
trust in them.

O Israel, trust in *Adonai,*
the One who is their help and their shield.

10 House of Aaron, trust in *Adonai,*
the One who is their help and their shield.
Believers, trust in *Adonai,*
the One who is their help and their shield.

Adonai has been mindful of us and will bless us.
May our God bless the House of Israel,
may our God bless the House of Aaron
May our God bless all believers, young or old,
May *Adonai* grant you increase,
you and all your children.

15 Blessed are you by *Adonai,* Maker of heaven and earth—

The heavens are *Adonai's* heavens—
but the earth God gave to human beings:
The dead cannot praise *Adonai,*
nor can all those whose lives have been silenced.
But we will bless *Adonai* now and forevermore—
HalleluYah!

PSALM 116

אָהַבְתִּי כִּי־יִשְׁמַע יְהוָה אֶת־קוֹלִי תַּחֲנוּנָי: 1

כִּי־הִטָּה אָזְנוֹ לִי וּבְיָמַי אֶקְרָא:

אֲפָפוּנִי חֶבְלֵי־מָוֶת וּמְצָרֵי שְׁאוֹל מְצָאוּנִי צָרָה וְיָגוֹן אֶמְצָא:

וּבְשֵׁם־יְהוָה אֶקְרָא אָנָּה יְהוָה מַלְּטָה נַפְשִׁי:

חַנּוּן יְהוָה וְצַדִּיק וֵאלֹהֵינוּ מְרַחֵם: 5

שֹׁמֵר פְּתָאיִם יְהוָה דַּלּוֹתִי וְלִי יְהוֹשִׁיעַ:

שׁוּבִי נַפְשִׁי לִמְנוּחָיְכִי כִּי־יְהוָה גָּמַל עָלָיְכִי:

כִּי חִלַּצְתָּ נַפְשִׁי מִמָּוֶת אֶת־עֵינִי מִן־דִּמְעָה אֶת־רַגְלִי מִדֶּחִי:

אֶתְהַלֵּךְ לִפְנֵי יְהוָה בְּאַרְצוֹת הַחַיִּים:

הֶאֱמַנְתִּי כִּי אֲדַבֵּר אֲנִי עָנִיתִי מְאֹד: 10

אֲנִי אָמַרְתִּי בְחָפְזִי כָּל־הָאָדָם כֹּזֵב:

מָה־אָשִׁיב לַיהוָה כָּל־תַּגְמוּלוֹהִי עָלָי:

כּוֹס־יְשׁוּעוֹת אֶשָּׂא וּבְשֵׁם יְהוָה אֶקְרָא:

נְדָרַי לַיהוָה אֲשַׁלֵּם נֶגְדָה־נָּא לְכָל־עַמּוֹ:

יָקָר בְּעֵינֵי יְהוָה הַמָּוְתָה לַחֲסִידָיו: 15

אָנָּה יְהוָה כִּי־אֲנִי עַבְדֶּךָ אֲנִי עַבְדְּךָ בֶּן־אֲמָתֶךָ

פִּתַּחְתָּ לְמוֹסֵרָי:

לְךָ־אֶזְבַּח זֶבַח תּוֹדָה וּבְשֵׁם יְהוָה אֶקְרָא:

נְדָרַי לַיהוָה אֲשַׁלֵּם נֶגְדָה־נָּא לְכָל־עַמּוֹ:

בְּחַצְרוֹת בֵּית יְהוָה בְּתוֹכֵכִי יְרוּשָׁלָ͏ִם הַלְלוּיָהּ:

PSALM 116

1 I love *Adonai,* who heard my voice and my supplication—
   who inclined an ear to me when I cried out.
   The cords of death encompassed me, the grave held me in
      its grip,
   I found myself in despair and anguish.
   I called out the Name *Adonai, "I beg You,* Adonai, *save my
      life!"*

5 *Adonai* is gracious and just; a God of great compassion
      who protects the humble:
   I was brought low, and *Adonai* saved me.
   Return, O my soul, to a sense of ease, for *Adonai* has dealt
      bountifully with you!
   For, my soul, you were saved from death—and my eyes
      from tears,
   my feet from stumbling:
   I will walk with *Adonai* in the land of the living.

10 Even when I said "I am in great pain," I still had faith—
   even when I so rashly said life is a mere illusion!
   Now what can I give back to *Adonai* for all *Adonai's*
      bounty to me?
   I will lift up the cup of deliverance—and call on the Name
      Adonai:
   fulfilling my vows to *Adonai* in the presence
   of all of God's people:

15 So dear in the eyes of *Adonai* are the death of the faithful:
   O *Adonai,* I am your servant, I am the child of your
      servant—
   You loosened my bonds.
   To You I offer Thanksgiving—on Your name, *Adonai,* I call:
   My vows to *Adonai* I fulfill in front of the whole nation—
      in the courtyard of the house of *Adonai,* in the
      heart of Jerusalem,
   Hallelu-Yah!

PSALM 117

1   הַלְלוּ אֶת־יְהֹוָה כָּל־גּוֹיִם שַׁבְּחוּהוּ כָּל־הָאֻמִּים:

כִּי גָבַר עָלֵינוּ חַסְדּוֹ וֶאֱמֶת־יְהֹוָה לְעוֹלָם הַלְלוּיָהּ:

PSALM 117

1 Praise *Adonai,* all nations—
Adore the Holy One, peoples of the world!
For the kindness of *Adonai* overwhelms us,
and *Adonai* is faithful forever!
Hallelu-Yah!

PSALM 118

1 הוֹדוּ לַיהוָה כִּי־טוֹב כִּי לְעוֹלָם חַסְדּוֹ:

יֹאמַר־נָא יִשְׂרָאֵל כִּי לְעוֹלָם חַסְדּוֹ:

יֹאמְרוּ נָא בֵית־אַהֲרֹן כִּי לְעוֹלָם חַסְדּוֹ:

יֹאמְרוּ נָא יִרְאֵי יְהוָה כִּי לְעוֹלָם חַסְדּוֹ:

5 מִן־הַמֵּצַר קָרָאתִי יָּהּ עָנָנִי בַמֶּרְחָב יָהּ:

יְהוָה לִי לֹא אִירָא מַה־יַּעֲשֶׂה לִי אָדָם:

יְהוָה לִי בְּעֹזְרָי וַאֲנִי אֶרְאֶה בְשֹׂנְאָי:

טוֹב לַחֲסוֹת בַּיהוָה מִבְּטֹחַ בָּאָדָם:

טוֹב לַחֲסוֹת בַּיהוָה מִבְּטֹחַ בִּנְדִיבִים:

10 כָּל־גּוֹיִם סְבָבוּנִי בְּשֵׁם יְהוָה כִּי אֲמִילַם:

סַבּוּנִי גַם־סְבָבוּנִי בְּשֵׁם יְהוָה כִּי אֲמִילַם:

סַבּוּנִי כִדְבוֹרִים דֹּעֲכוּ כְּאֵשׁ קוֹצִים בְּשֵׁם יְהוָה כִּי אֲמִילַם:

דָּחֹה דְחִיתַנִי לִנְפֹּל וַיהוָה עֲזָרָנִי:

עָזִּי וְזִמְרָת יָהּ וַיְהִי־לִי לִישׁוּעָה:

PSALM 118

1 Give thanks to *Adonai* who is good, whose kindness
   endures forever!
   Let Israel now say, "God's kindness is forever!"
   Let the House of Aaron now say, "God's kindness is
   forever!"
   Let *all* those who worship *Adonai* now say, "God's kindness
   is forever!"

5 I cried to God out of my distress and God answered me
   expansively—
   Adonai is with me. I have no fear—
   what can others do to me?
   Adonai is with me, the One Who helps me—I can face all
   my foes.
   It's better to seek shelter in *Adonai* than to trust human
   beings—
   Better to seek shelter in *Adonai* than to trust
   even the powerful—

10 All nations surrounded me, but in the name of *Adonai*
   I overcame them—
   They surrounded me on every side,
   but with the name of *Adonai* I overcame them—
   They surrounded me like swarming bees—
   but with the name of *Adonai* I overcame them.
   They pushed me like a fire that blazes through dry thorns,
   pushed me hard—
   I fell—but *Adonai* helped me—

PSALM 118 (*Continued*)

15 קוֹל רִנָּה וִישׁוּעָה בְּאָהֳלֵי צַדִּיקִים יְמִין יְהוָה עֹשָׂה חָיִל:

יְמִין יְהוָה רוֹמֵמָה יְמִין יְהוָה עֹשָׂה חָיִל:

לֹא אָמוּת כִּי־אֶחְיֶה וַאֲסַפֵּר מַעֲשֵׂי יָהּ:

יַסֹּר יִסְּרַנִּי יָּהּ וְלַמָּוֶת לֹא נְתָנָנִי:

פִּתְחוּ־לִי שַׁעֲרֵי־צֶדֶק אָבֹא־בָם אוֹדֶה יָהּ:

20 זֶה־הַשַּׁעַר לַיהוָה צַדִּיקִים יָבֹאוּ בוֹ:

אוֹדְךָ כִּי עֲנִיתָנִי וַתְּהִי־לִי לִישׁוּעָה:

אֶבֶן מָאֲסוּ הַבּוֹנִים הָיְתָה לְרֹאשׁ פִּנָּה:

מֵאֵת יְהוָה הָיְתָה זֹּאת הִיא נִפְלָאת בְּעֵינֵינוּ:

זֶה־הַיּוֹם עָשָׂה יְהוָה נָגִילָה וְנִשְׂמְחָה בוֹ:

25 אָנָּא יְהוָה הוֹשִׁיעָה נָּא אָנָּא יְהוָה הַצְלִיחָה נָּא:

בָּרוּךְ הַבָּא בְּשֵׁם יְהוָה בֵּרַכְנוּכֶם מִבֵּית יְהוָה:

אֵל יְהוָה וַיָּאֶר לָנוּ אִסְרוּ־חַג בַּעֲבֹתִים עַד קַרְנוֹת הַמִּזְבֵּחַ:

אֵלִי אַתָּה וְאוֹדֶךָּ אֱלֹהַי אֲרוֹמְמֶךָּ:

הוֹדוּ לַיהוָה כִּי־טוֹב כִּי לְעוֹלָם חַסְדּוֹ:

PSALM 118 (*Continued*)

15 *Adonai* is my strength and my song,
         Adonai is my deliverance—
     A song of joy echoes in the tents of the just—
     the right hand of *Adonai* does valiantly,
     when the right hand of *Adonai* is raised high,
         the right hand of *Adonai does* valiantly—
     I will not die but live
     so I can recount the deeds of *Adonai,*
     though the Holy One sorely chastened me, and
         I was given over to die.

     Open the gates of justice for me—so I may pass through
     and offer thanks to God!
20 This is the gate to *Adonai:* the just may enter here.
     I thank you, God,
     for You answered me,
     You were the source of my deliverance.
     The very stone that the builders rejected has become
     the chief cornerstone:
     This was *Adonai's* doing—how wondrous in our eyes!
     This is the day *Adonai* has made,
     let us rejoice and be glad in it!

25 Please, *Adonai,* continue to save us,
     please, *Adonai,* grant us success:
     Blessed are those who come in the name of *Adonai,*
     we bless you from the house of *Adonai:*
     Adonai is God, filling us with light—
     Bind the festival offering with ropes—lead it to the horns of
         the altar—
     You are my God and I thank You,
     O my God, I exalt You—
     Give thanks to *Adonai* who is good,
     Whose kindness is forever.

CHAPTER SEVEN

Frolicking with Leviathan:

Rosh Hodesh

The Hebrew word for "year," or *shanah*, suggests both change and returning or repeating. But the word for "month," *hodesh*, is related to new. On the Jewish calendar, every month is a new beginning, a chance to pray that the Holy One, the *Kadosh Barukh Hu*, will renew us, and all of our people, "for life and for peace, joy and gladness, deliverance and consolation."

The psalm for Rosh Hodesh, for the new month, captures that sense of newness and renewal in a way that reminds me of Miranda in Shakespeare's *The Tempest*, when she sees a whole slew of human beings for the very first time. "O brave new world that hast such people in it!" she exclaims, whereupon her more cynical, world-weary father Prospero responds, "'Tis new to *thee*." Reciting this psalm on each Rosh Hodesh frees us to celebrate Miranda's sense of utterly delighted wonder, and *pace* Prospero, to experience the world as new indeed to *us*.

The God of the creation story is like a Jewish mother—filling the world with all sorts of new creations, taking so much pleasure in everything that comes into being ("and God saw that it was good!") that She wants to create even more. "Eat, eat," God says to Adam. The qualities of *Adonai* in our Rosh Hodesh psalm echo the Creation story and at the same time, go robustly, wildly, eagerly beyond it. Robed in light, *Adonai* is at once the Interior

Decorator, Architect, Engineer, and Climatologist of the heavens, the earth, and all of the earth's contours and ecological systems. Thanks to *Adonai*, every little creature has a "local habitation"—birds can build nests and sing out from high among the branches of trees; lion cubs can snuggle at night in their dens; and gazelles can prance about on mountains. *Adonai* is the Source of all nourishment, as well, watering the world with springs and rivers and mountain tarns, so that grass grows to feed cattle, along with grains for human beings to turn into bread, and precious grapes, for wine. Most delightfully of all, the psalm for Rosh Hodesh celebrates *Adonai* as *playful*. God's world teems with fish and birds, lion cubs, gazelles, and little shrew mice—but God created Leviathan "to frolic with!"

The Rosh Hodesh psalm, celebrating the interdependence of all life and the place of each and every living creature on our planet, is an expression of what Abraham Joshua Heschel calls "radical amazement" at the beauty of God's world. But it is not naive. It ends in the same spirit as the breaking of the glass at weddings: an acknowledgement that beautiful as our world is and joyous as we may be; the world is still imperfect, and the hope remains that evil will be banished from the earth. Amen, and halleluyah!

PSALM 104

1 בָּרֲכִי נַפְשִׁי אֶת־יְהוָה יְהוָה אֱלֹהַי גָּדַלְתָּ מְּאֹד הוֹד
וְהָדָר לָבָשְׁתָּ:

עֹטֶה־אוֹר כַּשַּׂלְמָה נוֹטֶה שָׁמַיִם כַּיְרִיעָה:

הַמְקָרֶה בַמַּיִם עֲלִיּוֹתָיו הַשָּׂם־עָבִים רְכוּבוֹ הַמְהַלֵּךְ
עַל־כַּנְפֵי־רוּחַ:

עֹשֶׂה מַלְאָכָיו רוּחוֹת מְשָׁרְתָיו אֵשׁ לֹהֵט:

5 יָסַד־אֶרֶץ עַל־מְכוֹנֶיהָ בַּל־תִּמּוֹט עוֹלָם וָעֶד:

תְּהוֹם כַּלְּבוּשׁ כִּסִּיתוֹ עַל־הָרִים יַעַמְדוּ־מָיִם:

מִן־גַּעֲרָתְךָ יְנוּסוּן מִן־קוֹל רַעַמְךָ יֵחָפֵזוּן:

יַעֲלוּ הָרִים יֵרְדוּ בְקָעוֹת אֶל־מְקוֹם זֶה יָסַדְתָּ לָהֶם:

גְּבוּל־שַׂמְתָּ בַּל־יַעֲבֹרוּן בַּל־יְשׁוּבוּן לְכַסּוֹת הָאָרֶץ:

10 הַמְשַׁלֵּחַ מַעְיָנִים בַּנְּחָלִים בֵּין הָרִים יְהַלֵּכוּן:

יַשְׁקוּ כָּל־חַיְתוֹ שָׂדָי יִשְׁבְּרוּ פְרָאִים צְמָאָם:

עֲלֵיהֶם עוֹף־הַשָּׁמַיִם יִשְׁכּוֹן מִבֵּין עֳפָאיִם יִתְּנוּ־קוֹל:

מַשְׁקֶה הָרִים מֵעֲלִיּוֹתָיו מִפְּרִי מַעֲשֶׂיךָ תִּשְׂבַּע הָאָרֶץ:

מַצְמִיחַ חָצִיר לַבְּהֵמָה וְעֵשֶׂב לַעֲבֹדַת הָאָדָם
לְהוֹצִיא לֶחֶם מִן־הָאָרֶץ:

PSALM 104

1   Bless *Adonai,* O my soul,
        Adonai, my God, You are very great—
     With majestic glory Your garment, You
     dress in light like a robe
     and hang the heavens like drapes;
     from the upper waters You fashion beams for Your chamber,
     turning the clouds into a chariot, riding on wings of the
        wind.
     You turn the winds into messengers, into blazing angels of
        fire,

5   as You set the earth on a site from which it will never be
        shaken.

     Once, deep seas covered the land like a cloak—
     the waters stood over mountains—
     You rebuked them, and they fled—from the sound of Your
        thunder
     they hurried away,
     they rose up the mountains, they sank down into valleys—
     into the very places You arranged for them,
     within the boundaries
     You chose.
     So that never again would they cover the earth,

10   You send springs into rivers and flowing mountain streams—
     the wild animals all drink—wild asses
     slake their thirst.
     Birds of the sky rest above them and send out their song
        from branches of trees.
     You make grass grow to feed cattle,
     and You make grain so human beings
     can bring forth bread from the earth,
     sustaining the human heart.

PSALM 104 (*Continued*)

15 וְיַיִן יְשַׂמַּח לְבַב־אֱנוֹשׁ לְהַצְהִיל פָּנִים מִשָּׁמֶן וְלֶחֶם
לְבַב־אֱנוֹשׁ יִסְעָד:

יִשְׂבְּעוּ עֲצֵי יְהֹוָה אַרְזֵי לְבָנוֹן אֲשֶׁר נָטָע:

אֲשֶׁר־שָׁם צִפֳּרִים יְקַנֵּנוּ חֲסִידָה בְּרוֹשִׁים בֵּיתָהּ:

הָרִים הַגְּבֹהִים לַיְּעֵלִים סְלָעִים מַחְסֶה לַשְׁפַנִּים:

עָשָׂה יָרֵחַ לְמוֹעֲדִים שֶׁמֶשׁ יָדַע מְבוֹאוֹ:

20 תָּשֶׁת חֹשֶׁךְ וִיהִי לָיְלָה בּוֹ־תִרְמֹשׂ כָּל־חַיְתוֹ־יָעַר:

הַכְּפִירִים שֹׁאֲגִים לַטָּרֶף וּלְבַקֵּשׁ מֵאֵל אָכְלָם:

תִּזְרַח הַשֶּׁמֶשׁ יֵאָסֵפוּן וְאֶל־מְעוֹנֹתָם יִרְבָּצוּן:

יֵצֵא אָדָם לְפָעֳלוֹ וְלַעֲבֹדָתוֹ עֲדֵי־עָרֶב:

מָה־רַבּוּ מַעֲשֶׂיךָ יְהֹוָה כֻּלָּם בְּחָכְמָה עָשִׂיתָ
מָלְאָה הָאָרֶץ קִנְיָנֶךָ:

25 זֶה הַיָּם גָּדוֹל וּרְחַב יָדָיִם שָׁם רֶמֶשׂ וְאֵין מִסְפָּר חַיּוֹת
קְטַנּוֹת עִם־גְּדֹלוֹת:

שָׁם אֳנִיּוֹת יְהַלֵּכוּן לִוְיָתָן זֶה יָצַרְתָּ לְשַׂחֶק־בּוֹ:

כֻּלָּם אֵלֶיךָ יְשַׂבֵּרוּן לָתֵת אָכְלָם בְּעִתּוֹ:

תִּתֵּן לָהֶם יִלְקֹטוּן תִּפְתַּח יָדְךָ יִשְׂבְּעוּן טוֹב:

תַּסְתִּיר פָּנֶיךָ יִבָּהֵלוּן תֹּסֵף רוּחָם יִגְוָעוּן וְאֶל־עֲפָרָם יְשׁוּבוּן:

PSALM 104 (*Continued*)

15 You make wine to gladden the human heart,
   to make faces glisten as if from oil.
   The trees of *Adonai* drink their fill—the cedars of Lebanon
     God planted—
   birds build their nests there, and storks
   make their home amid cypress.
   High mountains are for the gazelles, cliffs of rock
   shelter the little shrew mouse.

   You made the moon to measure the seasons; the sun knows
     when to set.

20 You bring down darkness, and there is night,
   all the beasts of the forest stir,
   young lions roar for their prey, seeking food from You
   until, at daylight, they regroup,
   go back to their dens to lie down,
   just as people go out to work
   to labor until evening.

   How great are Your works, *Adonai:* You fashioned all life
     with wisdom,
   The earth is filled with Your creations!

25 Here is the sea, great and wide, where ships sail—
   It teems with creatures—small ones and large—
   There is Leviathan
   You fashioned to frolic with!

   All of them look to You to provide food in its season.
   When You offer it, they gather it up
   when You open Your hand,
   they are well satisfied.

   But they panic when You hide Your face
   and when You take away their breath, they perish—
   they return to the dust from whence they've come.

PSALM 104 (*Continued*)

30 תְּשַׁלַּח רוּחֲךָ יִבָּרֵאוּן וּתְחַדֵּשׁ פְּנֵי אֲדָמָה:

יְהִי כְבוֹד יְהוָה לְעוֹלָם יִשְׂמַח יְהוָה בְּמַעֲשָׂיו:

הַמַּבִּיט לָאָרֶץ וַתִּרְעָד יִגַּע בֶּהָרִים וְיֶעֱשָׁנוּ:

אָשִׁירָה לַיהוָה בְּחַיָּי אֲזַמְּרָה לֵאלֹהַי בְּעוֹדִי:

יֶעֱרַב עָלָיו שִׂיחִי אָנֹכִי אֶשְׂמַח בַּיהוָה:

35 יִתַּמּוּ חַטָּאִים מִן־הָאָרֶץ וּרְשָׁעִים עוֹד אֵינָם בָּרֲכִי נַפְשִׁי

אֶת־יְהוָה הַלְלוּיָהּ:

PSALM 104 (*Continued*)

30 With Your breath, life is created; You renew the face of the
earth.
   May the glory of *Adonai* endure forever,
   may *Adonai* rejoice forever in these works,
   Who makes the world tremble
   merely by looking,
   Who touches the mountains, and they smoke.

   I will sing to *Adonai* as long as I live, all my life I will sing
      praises to God
   May my words be sweet to the Eternal One. As for me,
      I rejoice in *Adonai*

35 May transgressors vanish from the earth and the wicked be
no more.

   O my soul, bless *Adonai,* Praise be to God, *Hallelu-Yah.*

CHAPTER EIGHT

A *Heart of Flesh, a Heart of Courage*:

Psalm for the Season of Repentance

Though Ps 27 is recited every day during *Elul*—the month leading up to Rosh Hashanah and Yom Kippur—until the end of the festival of Sukkot, the psalm really isn't about what its liturgical context might lead one to assume. It is not, for example, about self-abasement; it is not a confession of sin, an admission of guilt, a litany of *Al Het* ("For the sin we have sinned before You . . ."), as on Rosh Hashanah and Yom Kippur.

What then is it? Ps 27 is a most tender expression of trust, an expression of deep yearning. It is a prayer of such emotional and spiritual vulnerability that it seems a fulfillment of God's promise to Ezekiel, "I will take away their heart of stone . . . and give them a heart of flesh" (11:18), for who but someone with a "heart of flesh" could cry out to God, "my heart yearns for You to seek me?"

If we allow ourselves to take the first two lines of Ps 27 seriously, it truly is a profoundly *comforting* psalm. So many of us have "little" fears; not the fear of global warming or the fear of an imminent earthquake, but the fear of feeling foolish or stupid, the fear of making a mistake, of not being liked, of being thought unlovable. What happens to our experience of all of our personal fears, if we practice the art of "Holy Reading" and repeat the first two lines of this psalm, over and over again, until it assumes a deeply personal meaning and we make it, truly, our own?

Indeed, line after line in the psalm calls to us to make them our own. They make me, for example, think about how *Adonai* has been my "light" and my "help"—helping me become aware of difficult realities I otherwise might not have wanted to see and then helping me *not* fall apart when, finally, I face them. In another key entirely: my "light" through the mitzvot, for especially through the practice of Shabbat, for wonders of order, holiness, peace, and community have opened to me. What about you? From what fears are you released, might you be released through a faith in *Adonai*? What light can you envision God casting upon *your* life?

You need not attend synagogue daily to recite this psalm every day between the first of *Elul* and the end of Sukkot—or you can recite it out of its liturgical context entirely—for it can be a powerful and transformative spiritual exercise at any time of year. After all, do we not all long for strength, long for hope, and long to have "a heart of courage" every day of our life?

PSALM 27

1 לְדָוִד יְהוָה אוֹרִי וְיִשְׁעִי מִמִּי אִירָא יְהוָה מָעוֹז חַיַּי
מִמִּי אֶפְחָד:

בִּקְרֹב עָלַי מְרֵעִים לֶאֱכֹל אֶת־בְּשָׂרִי צָרַי וְאֹיְבַי לִי הֵמָּה
כָּשְׁלוּ וְנָפָלוּ:

אִם־תַּחֲנֶה עָלַי מַחֲנֶה לֹא־יִירָא לִבִּי אִם־תָּקוּם עָלַי מִלְחָמָה
בְּזֹאת אֲנִי בוֹטֵחַ:

אַחַת שָׁאַלְתִּי מֵאֵת־יְהוָה אוֹתָהּ אֲבַקֵּשׁ שִׁבְתִּי בְּבֵית־יְהוָה
כָּל־יְמֵי חַיַּי לַחֲזוֹת בְּנֹעַם־יְהוָה וּלְבַקֵּר בְּהֵיכָלוֹ:

5 כִּי יִצְפְּנֵנִי בְּסֻכֹּה בְּיוֹם רָעָה יַסְתִּרֵנִי בְּסֵתֶר אָהֳלוֹ
בְּצוּר יְרוֹמְמֵנִי:

וְעַתָּה יָרוּם רֹאשִׁי עַל־אֹיְבַי סְבִיבוֹתַי וְאֶזְבְּחָה בְאָהֳלוֹ זִבְחֵי
תְרוּעָה אָשִׁירָה וַאֲזַמְּרָה לַיהוָה:

שְׁמַע־יְהוָה קוֹלִי אֶקְרָא וְחָנֵּנִי וַעֲנֵנִי:

לְךָ אָמַר לִבִּי בַּקְּשׁוּ פָנָי אֶת־פָּנֶיךָ יְהוָה אֲבַקֵּשׁ:

אַל־תַּסְתֵּר פָּנֶיךָ מִמֶּנִּי אַל תַּט־בְּאַף עַבְדֶּךָ עֶזְרָתִי הָיִיתָ
אַל־תִּטְּשֵׁנִי וְאַל־תַּעַזְבֵנִי אֱלֹהֵי יִשְׁעִי:

PSALM 27

1 *For David.*
   Adonai is my light and my help, whom should I fear?
   Adonai is my source of strength, who can frighten me?
   Though those who wish me harm draw near to devour me
       these foes, these enemies—
   they stumble and fall.
   If they surrounded me on all sides,
   still my heart would be fearless—
   If they warred on me,
   I would still trust.
   I have just one request of *Adonai*—
       for this I yearn—
   Let me dwell in the house of *Adonai* all the days of my life,
   let me gaze on the loveliness of *Adonai,* in God's sanctuary.

5 For God will hide me in a shelter when times are evil,
   concealing me in God's own tent, standing me high on a
       rock
   to raise my head above all the enemies around me:
   I will make offerings to God in that tent, shouting for joy,
   singing and chanting praise of *Adonai*

   O hear my voice, *Adonai,* when I call You—
   be gracious to me—
   answer me—my heart yearns for You
   to seek me. It is Your face that I seek—
   O God, do not hide Your face from me in anger—
   do not turn away from me—
   You have been my help always,
   do not abandon me—don't leave me,
   O God Who saves me.

PSALM 27 (*Continued*)

10 כִּי־אָבִי וְאִמִּי עֲזָבוּנִי וַיהוָה יַאַסְפֵנִי:

הוֹרֵנִי יְהוָה דַּרְכֶּךָ וּנְחֵנִי בְּאֹרַח מִישׁוֹר לְמַעַן שׁוֹרְרָי:

אַל־תִּתְּנֵנִי בְּנֶפֶשׁ צָרָי כִּי קָמוּ־בִי עֵדֵי־שֶׁקֶר וִיפֵחַ חָמָס:

לוּלֵא הֶאֱמַנְתִּי לִרְאוֹת בְּטוּב־יְהוָה בְּאֶרֶץ חַיִּים:

קַוֵּה אֶל־יְהוָה חֲזַק וְיַאֲמֵץ לִבֶּךָ וְקַוֵּה אֶל־יְהוָה:

PSALM 27 (*Continued*)

10 Though my father and mother leave me, *Adonai* will gather
    me in.
    Teach me Your way, *Adonai,*
    by leading me on a straight path
    to confound my foes. Don't give me over to them,
    false witnesses
    who have risen against me,
    whose every breath is violence.

    Let me believe
    I will see the goodness of *Adonai*
        in this land of the living—
    and I will hope in *Adonai*—
    Be strong, have
    a heart of courage,
    and hope in *Adonai*!

CHAPTER NINE

Glowing in the Nuptial Light:

The Psalms of *Kabbalat Shabbat*

"God blessed the seventh day" . . . (Gen 2:3) God blessed it with the light of a human face: the light on someone's face during the week is not the same as it is on the Sabbath. (Gen. Rab. 11, 2)

After six days of getting and spending, of immersion in everyday life, we come to that moment in the week that asks us to let go, to prepare ourselves for the transition from ordinary time to sacred time, to ready ourselves for Shabbat. The Zohar teaches us during the week, "strict Judgment rules and all judgments are aroused," but on Shabbat, "all judgments are suppressed, and pleasure and joy abound"; a holy "breath of delight" spreads through "all those who observe the Sabbath."[11] Sometimes the very prospect of Shabbat helps us let go of the demands, details, tensions of the past six days; we welcome Shabbat rest with a sigh of relief. Inevitably, though, there are other times in which our minds and hearts are too preoccupied, our worries too persistent; it feels like we just have *so* much to do—how can we *possibly* ease ourselves into the sense of tranquility that is the promise of the Sabbath?

And what, after all, does entering Shabbat—sacred time—really mean? What does it really ask of us? What are the qualities of the Holy One who is calling us to welcome and honor the Day of

[11]*The Wisdom of the Zohar: An Anthology of Texts*, vol. 3, arr. by Isaiah Tishby, trans. David Goldstein (Oxford: Littman Library of Jewish Civilization, 1991), pp. 1281, 1283.

Rest? Whether we chant the psalms of *Kabbalat Shabbat* in a communal or a private setting, sometimes singing aloud, sometimes whispering to ourselves, the answers to those questions subtly unfold. The psalms reveal how profoundly Shabbat is a time for healing for both ourselves and our world. For the kabbalists of Safed, who originated the *Kabbalat Shabbat* service at the end of the sixteenth century,[12] that healing was envisioned as a kind of cosmic marriage. The ruptures and divisions of ordinary life dissolve, as the opening six psalms—one for each day of the preceding week—build in intensity to celebrate the sovereignty of God in ourselves as individuals, over the people Israel, and ultimately over the universe as a whole. The sequence of the psalms is meant to prepare the ground for that cosmic marriage—that experience of wholeness and healing—by opening our souls truly to feel the Presence of the Divine, the Shekhinah. The Shekhinah, in the tradition, is envisioned as a radiant and beloved Bride, a Queen, in the climactic hymn of *Kabbalat Shabbat*, *L'kha Dodi*—"Come, my Beloved."

PSALM 95

Whether the transition to sacred time is easy or difficult, as we begin with Ps 95, each of us discovers that our tradition recognizes how profound a challenge readiness for Shabbat can be.

No matter how many times one prays or reads or sings this psalm, its last lines always seem to come as a shock or at the very least, to be spiritually unsettling. Opening with a call for collective, joyous, praise, going on to celebrate the reign of *Adonai* in the universe, Ps 95 seems to veer at the end to a stern, disturbing, message. We feel how disturbing it is particularly in its liturgical context, the first psalm of *Kabbalat Shabbat*. As we ready ourselves for "the day of rest," why should we be reminded of our

---

[12]The very first record we have of the mystics' *Kabbalat Shabbat* service is in the *Seder HaYom* by Rabbi Moshe ben Makhir (1599).

ancient ancestors whom God swore "would never come to My
place of rest?"

"From One Extreme to the Other" in the Psalm

To begin with, the psalm as a whole seems to move from one
extreme to the other: welcoming us, then seeking to awe us, seeking to humble us, and finally, issuing a dark warning. On the one
hand, the psalm emphasizes the sovereignty of *Adonai* in our
world, a major theme for the kabbalists. It calls on us to acknowledge the greatness of the Holy One, to express gratitude for
God's care, and to follow God's laws. But on the other, it maps a
process of our growing intimacy with *Adonai*. Yet the closer we
get, the more challenging the message.

The psalm begins by inviting us to sing out, make noise—to
robustly and joyfully celebrate God, like pilgrims and Levites at
the Temple in ancient Jerusalem. It continues with expressions
of gratitude and with recognition of God's wondrous role as Creator of our world, from the grandest heights to the deepest
depths, the mountain peaks to the innards of the earth. But then
the choreography suddenly shifts. Instead of our dancing and
singing, the call goes out for us, like those ancient pilgrims, to
bow and to kneel—to prostrate ourselves—in humility before
Adonai, to acknowledge the vastness of God's sovereign power.
We're asked to see ourselves as humble sheep who should put
their trust in their Shepherd.

And then there is yet another radical shift. We who are reciting or singing or chanting or whispering the psalm, are suddenly
speaking in the voice of God, recalling the failure of our ancestors, newly liberated from slavery, to enter the Promised Land.
"Do not harden your hearts": as we speak those words, we are
warning ourselves, as God warns us, of the barriers we can erect
between ourselves and God.

Taken as a whole, Ps 95 speaks to our pride and our humility,
our shame and our promise, our error—and our glory. Most mov-

ingly of all, as we will see, it suggests to us that how the Holy One is depends solely on how we ourselves relate to the Holy One.

Singing it Together, Praying it Alone

The first psalm of the *Kabbalat Shabbat* opens with an invitation: it calls for *all* worshippers to join together to sing songs and make music praising God, recognizing God's greatness, God's creation of the world, God's ultimate rule. In congregational settings, there are many stirringly beautiful melodies to which the words, *Lekhu Neranenah* (*Come, let us sing gladly*) have been set, and the psalm comes alive in a particular way when we sing it with others. In the Hebrew, four verbs in the first two lines alone begin with the letter *nuhn*, the indicator for "us." For in Ps 95, when we raise our voices in community, *we become the very worshipers to whom the psalm is calling: we are the "us" singing gladly*; we're welcoming *one another* to join the throng of praise for God. We are all, as it were, pilgrims at the Temple. In the process, God truly becomes our "Rock," in the sense of becoming the singular, divine, stable, center to whom we are all singing.

The "Rock" as Still Center

Imagining God as "Rock" can be comforting—especially if the week has been difficult, draining, hectic, demanding, chaotic, filled with more challenges than we would like. Oh, for a still center! For something strong and unchanging to which to cling, against which to lean! During the week, many of us may be glad to have the spiritual energy, imagination, time or space that enables us to sense the Holy One's presence in our lives as the symbol of profound stability, a "Rock."

But this is not everyday. It is Erev Shabbat, the Sabbath eve. As the psalm continues and as our voices move over the words of the psalm—that silent Rock becomes more present, more alive. *For every psalm, every prayer, is an act of relationship, a way of moving into holy Presence, a way of opening ourselves to hear the voice of the Divine, which the cares of ordinary life may, all too frequently, muffle.* Ultimately, we'll see that the image of the "Rock" evokes a whole spectrum of emotion—from fear to faith.

From Sacred Space to Sacred Time

"Come, let us bow and kneel before, let us worship, our Maker, *Adonai*": as we speak that next line, the tenor of the psalm changes. In most congregations, if we have been singing or speaking aloud together, now is the time we lower our voices, recite the words to ourselves. Even if we are alone, we can change our tone, even whisper.

For the nearly one thousand years that a Temple stood in Jerusalem, these words may well have served as a kind of stage direction, an invitation. As the Levites sang, "Come, let us bow and kneel . . . ," the gathered pilgrims would have prostrated themselves to God in the precincts of that sacred space. Ever since the fall of the Second Temple nearly two millennia ago, however, it is sacred *time* rather than sacred *space* that is the center of spiritual experience for us. "Judaism is a religion of time," as theologian Abraham Joshua Heschel has taught us, "aiming at the sanctification of time. . . . Judaism teaches us to be attached to holiness in time."[13] It is *Shabbat* which is holy, not our prayer-space.

". . . let us bow . . ."

How are we to enter this sanctified time? What happens when we do? The words "Come, let us bow and kneel" suggest that to

---

[13]In *The Sabbath: Its Meaning for Modern Man* (New York: Farrar, Straus and Giroux, 1951), p. 8.

experience a sense of sanctity is first to awaken a sense of humili-ty. For it is only in moments of humility that a voice of spiritual power can emerge not from our egos, which seek to be in con-trol, but from a deeper place within us. To acknowledge the need for humility now is to take the words of the psalm seriously: that is, to actually *do* what the words say, marking the words with a physical gesture.

For example, instead of just *saying* the words, what if we actu-ally *do* bow our heads[14] before "*Adonai* our Maker," and in that moment let ourselves actually *feel* the resonance of calling our God *our* "Maker," as well as Maker of the universe, of worlds upon worlds, Maker of earth's mountain peaks, of vast seas and finally, of the very ground we are standing on? If we take the time to experience that moment of awe, that sense of humility before the grandeur of God, we can open ourselves as well to feel the power of the image that follows. The twenty-third psalm opens by declaring "*Adonai* is my shepherd"; a similar image is invoked here in Ps 95, when we say, we are "the people in God's pasture, the flock in God's hand." The difference, of course, is that in the former, we emphasize God-as-shepherd; in the latter, we-as-sheep. And therein lies the difficulty: after the *Shoah* (Holocaust), many of us may find the very thought problematic, even disturbing. To speak of the Jewish people as like "sheep" is to arouse associations with victimization, with a frightening pas-sivity. Further, many of us like to—need to—think of ourselves as "captains of our ship," in charge of our lives; go-getters. The culture most often rewards us for that attitude, regards it as healthy. We are self-reliant. Why would we *want* to see ourselves as like "sheep" in "God's hands?"

---

[14]There is a fascinating, highly detailed discussion of the spiritual significance of bowing (and other nonverbal aspects of prayer) in Uri Ehrlich's *The Nonverbal Language of Prayer: Texts and Studies in Ancient Judaism*, trans. Dena Ordan (Tubingen, Germany: Mohr Siebeck, 2004).

Because, above all, it is not an image of passivity—it is an image of *trust*.

Entering Sacred Time

Why "trust" and why does it matter? The answers come in the section that follows: *Do not harden your hearts,* we say, speaking the words we imagine God speaking to us, as if it is a voice from both within us and beyond us.

Do not harden your hearts . . . In ancient times, that line may have been spoken by a Levite in the Temple, urging the people to learn from the lesson of the past, when our ancestors wandered in the wilderness. Today, in many congregations, the line is sung collectively, as if the congregation as a whole is echoing the voice of the Holy One and evoking the biblical world of the past. At the same time, the words can have a penetrating power when we recite them to ourselves alone.

For the lines cast us into the world of ancestral memory. Despite their having witnessed the miracle of liberation from slavery and the parting of the sea, the ancient Hebrews were repeatedly harrowed by fear and despair in their desert wanderings. Having lost the familiar, they are terrified in the face of the unknown. Every setback or challenge they encounter, they experience as threatening total disaster, and the only solution they come up with is to run away, run back. The specific incident at Merivah and Massah referred to in Ps 95 is described in *Parashat Beshallah*, in the book of Exodus:

> The people quarreled with Moses. "Give us water to drink," they said; and Moses replied to them, "Why do you quarrel with me? Why do you try *Adonai*?" But the people thirsted there for water; and the people grumbled against Moses and said, "Why did you bring us up from Egypt, to kill our children and livestock with thirst?"
>
> Moses cried out to *Adonai*, saying "What shall I do with this people? Before long they will be stoning me!" Then *Adonai*

said to Moses, "Pass before the people; take with you some of the elders of Israel, and take along the rod with which you struck the Nile and set out. I will be standing there before you on the rock at Horeb. Strike the rock and water will issue from it, and the people will drink."

And Moses did so in the sight of the elders of Israel. The place was named Massah ["Trial"] and Merivah ["Quarrel"], because the Israelites quarreled and tried *Adonai*, saying, "Is *Adonai* present among us or not?" (Exod 17:2–7)

Thirsty, the people are querulous and angry, attacking Moses for liberating them to begin with and questioning the very reality of God. Yet it is not the physical *thirst* that motivates the attack — it is their *fear*. They have no idea how to cope with the new reality of the desert wilderness, the new reality in which they are called upon to trust Moses, trust life, trust God.

Do not harden your hearts . . . comes the psalmist's expression of God's own anguish and anger with the generation of slaves. That anguish is intensified in the original Hebrew where the word for "I swore," *nish*ba'ti, rhymes with *be'*appi, "my wrath." But it also rhymes with *menuḥati*, "my peace," "my place of rest." Through these rhymes, the psalm is urging us to be different from that slave generation. It is urging us not to be pulled back into the past, to trust the present, and to trust what is to come.

The men and women of the desert generation died in the desert, never to enter the Promised Land, the place where freedom and holiness kiss. Why should we, moments before the onset of Shabbat, be compared to them? Because we, too, are in liminal space. We are on the brink of leaving the workaday week — where our lives are ruled by getting and spending, achieving, acquiring, performing, competing, rushing, proving — and entering Shabbat, a "cathedral in time." *Do not harden your hearts:* don't be afraid of *not* working for a whole day, *not* shopping, *not* checking e-mail, *not* achieving, *not* turning on the TV.

At the very moment that we chant the climactic ending words of the psalm, *I swore that never would they come to My place of rest*, we ourselves have the possibility of leaving the past behind—the past of our ancestors *and* the past of our own week. We can let go. We can ready ourselves spiritually to enter our version of the "place of rest," the place of sanctified time, a new state of being: Shabbat rest. We can sing a new song to God.

PSALM 96

Opening with a summons to us to praise, our second psalm of the *Kabbalat Shabbat* service is a poem of imperatives, an explosion of rapture that reaches beyond the confines of ourselves, our community, our synagogue; beyond our own people, in praise of God's sovereignty in the universe. It is also, above all, an invitation to discover an aspect of our relationship to God we may never have experienced or expressed before. It is an invitation to let go of whatever "melody" dominated our week and find the melody of our Shabbat. "Sing a new song!" says the psalm— express one's own song, express *our* own song, consider again and anew at this very moment what God has created; find new and marvelous wonders in our world *now*. From the oceans teeming with life to the forests thick with trees, God's creative energy ignites every corner of the world.

Seven times in the course of the psalm we sing out the word "all," for Ps 96 reaches out in the fullness of joy to honor the divine energy that infuses and encompasses the whole world and everything—and everyone—within it. The psalm calls to everyone, to people of all faiths, to join us in celebrating God's Presence and God's rule.

And to do more than celebrate: it bids us come closer to God. In an image drawn from the architecture of the ancient Temple, the psalm asks us to come into God's "sacred space," the Temple's courtyard, with our "offering." In congregational settings, we may just sing those words in a rousing melody. But if we are praying this psalm on our own, the line gives us a profound opportunity to ask ourselves what, in these moments before Shabbat, *our* "offering" to God can be. As we bid farewell to the past week and prepare to enter Shabbat, *what gift can we bring, what gift are we bringing, to God?* Is it, for example, an expression of gratitude for our health, for our loved ones, for a moment of joy we experienced, a moment of sheer wonder? Is it a letting go of a regret, or a grudge, or a resentment, that served as a kind of hard crust on our heart? Is it a piece of music, a poem of praise? is it a prayer? In the words of Ps 116, as we enter Shabbat can we ask ourselves, "What can I give back to God, for all God's bounty to me?"

In Ps 96, the attributes of *Adonai* that we are celebrating go beyond even those of God's glory, God's radiance, God's bountiful creativity. Crucially, God for us here is also the promise of a just order in the world: "God judges all peoples fairly." Despite the messiness of our all-too-human world, despite the chaos and tension we sometimes feel around us, the great discovery that awaits us in the courtyard of *Adonai* is that there *is* an ultimate stability, justice, and an ultimate rectitude we can rely upon: the foundations of the world are firm and will not falter. Although we are all aware of the reality of imperfection, in the end, the psalm declares, God's Truth will triumph.

In a marvelous work called *Pirkei Shira*, known in English as "The Song of the Universe" and originally compiled sometime from the fifth century to the seventh century, all of Creation — the heavens; earth; desert; streams; sun, moon, and stars; wind; fig, apple, and pomegranate trees; a sheaf of barley and a sheaf of wheat; eagles, hens, cranes, and swallows; the great whale, the bear, the fly; truly, *everything*, in Creation is eternally singing to the Creator: in Jewish tradition, the universe as a whole is alive with the sound of music! That is the message of the end of this psalm: just as we are singing "a new song," so all of creation itself is singing, exulting in the ideals of justice and the joy of God's

Presence in the world. It is a world in harmony—musically and spiritually.[15]

PSALM 97

In most synagogues, a hush falls upon the congregation as we move from Ps 96 to Ps 97, which is most often recited to oneself. The rabbis of the Talmud teach us that the words of a prayer linger on our lips after we have recited them. Ps 97 feels like that lingering, for the words, thoughts, and images of the psalm echo those we encountered earlier. It is as if, in Ps 97, we are gathering up all the holy sparks of energy ignited by our celebration of God in order to set the spiritual stage for the entrance of the Shekhinah.

The revelation of the sovereignty of God

Ps 96 began and ended with an ecstatic invitation to the whole planet to rejoice along with a promise, a vision, an exultant expectation: divine judgment is coming; true justice and ultimate truth are soon to make their presence felt on earth. Now whether we are in synagogue or at home, with others or on our own, we move into a quieter space—and yet as we do, the psalm calls upon us to experience an even greater joy. Psalm 96 urged us to declare God as Sovereign of our universe; in Ps 97, we do it. "*Adonai* reigns," we proclaim. In a foretaste of the messianic age in which God will rule the world, at this moment on Shabbat *God is here.*

The impact of God's sovereignty

God is here—but there's no halcyon description of a lion celebrating the reign of God by lying down with a baby lamb! Instead, the psalm offers us numinous, even terrifying, images of a world-changing storm; complete with fiery bolts of lightning, a trembling earth, and mountains that are collapsing like melting wax. Why might that be so?

[15]I am grateful to Rabbi Joel Rembaum for that suggestion.

One way I suggest we understand the ferocity of these images is by asking ourselves how it would feel for each one of us to acknowledge fully that there truly *is* an ultimate order reigning over our own lives and over our whole universe, and *that ultimate order is here, now.* What would it feel like for our body, mind, heart, and spirit to experience the truth and the reality of the Presence of the Holy One here, now? Would our insistently controlling egos not find themselves "melting like wax?" Would we not, like the earth as a whole, tremble? Would the recognition not shatter our familiar worlds, like the lightning bolts shattering the sky?

The Impact of God's Sovereignty on Zion

Crucially, though, whether we are praying this psalm in a congregation or we are praying it on our own, the psalm itself reassures us that we are not alone. As ego-shattering an experience as the full acknowledgement of God's Presence and rule may be, from the point of view of this psalm we are not selves or souls cast adrift in desperate prayer before an implacable God. The lightning roars, the mountains melt, but "Zion hears and rejoices! The towns of Judah exult!" If as Jews we celebrate God "with all our heart, and with all our soul, and with all our might," as we say in our *Shema* prayer, we also celebrate the presence and righteousness of the living God. Our tradition insists that the ways of God are just; that goodness and truth will triumph in the world despite all the moral maelstroms, the outbreaks of evil. We have been given a Torah to honor and to follow, a pathway through the bewilderment and confusion of life: God's Law.

"Light is Sown for the Righteous"

But what is the relationship of each of us to God and God's Law? What values truly inform our lives? What values are expressed in our actions? Like a zoom lens, the psalm now narrows its focus and addresses each of us directly. To claim to love

God and God's ways is not enough. "You who love *Adonai*, hate evil!" the psalm demands, forcing us, even as we say the words, to become aware of our responsibilities as moral beings and as Jews.

To assume that responsibility is less of a burden, however, than a precious gift. For the psalm now subtly reverses the grim warning we heard in Ps 95: by making the choice at this very moment not to be among those whose "hearts stray," we can awaken our hearts to a new sense of trust, to an awareness of God's loving protection. In Ps 96, we sang out that God is coming to rule all the world with *tzedek*; we said that *tzedek* is the very foundation of God's throne; we bid the heavens themselves declare the *tzedek* of God. Now, as we move to the culminating lines of the psalm, *tzedek* is transformed into *tzadik*, the kind of person the psalm urges us to become, men and women whose very being embody the good, that "hate evil," and are truly righteous.

To undergo that transformation is to experience the "dark clouds" dissolve. In our mystical tradition, the light that begins to shine now, this new and holy light, is a nuptial light—the light of the Holy One joining the Shekhinah; it is the unfathomable Deity becoming Presence. "Light is sown for the righteous and joy for the upright of heart." A new joy, a new wholeness, a new sense of peace. A new song to *Adonai*!

PSALM 98

"Rejoice!" we ended Ps 97, and indeed that is just what we do in Ps 98. The psalm is a celebration of the *yeshua:* the saving power of *Adonai*.

One way to grasp the idea of God's "saving power" is to see it from the collective, tradition-rich point of view. The image of God's "holy arm" inevitably evokes the "outstretched arm" that we speak of at Passover: God triumphed over Pharaoh, split the sea, and brought the children of Israel from slavery to freedom. If we look at the image in this fashion, it is like we are coming full circle. For let us recall that the psalm with which we began the *Kab-*

balat Shabbat series, Ps 95, chastised the generation of liberated slaves for their stubborn lack of faith, and told us sternly that God gave up on them—despised them in fact for their hard hearts.

But what's happened now? A few psalms later, and there has been a transformation. We have been welcoming our Sovereign God into our midst; we have been celebrating the rule of holiness and justice in our world; singing and shouting with joy to the Divine Presence. *We have, in other words, dissociated ourselves from the generation of those with "hard hearts."*

God's triumph was revealed at the Red Sea, but the story scarcely ended there. As we speak or sing or murmur the words of Ps 98, we can see God's victory over the forces of oppression and, at the same time, continue the ancient story: the story of how God has "kept faith" with Israel. In the story in our Torah, God "kept the faith" by bringing us to Sinai and *giving* us Torah. If God kept the faith with us, can we not keep faith with God? The generation of slaves could not enter the sacred space of the Promised Land, but we can reaffirm our Covenant with God by entering fully into our sacred time. The door opens fully now, to Shabbat.

As if to acknowledge and herald our triumph over the past— the past of our people and our own past week—we call out for a burst of music: the music of the human voice, bursting into "songs of praise" as we are now; the music of the ancient Temple instruments—lyres, trumpets, horns; and ultimately, the music of all of *nature* itself. We are calling upon the very planet to celebrate *Adonai*: the sea and all the sea-creatures roar; the rivers clap their hands; mountains sing. Indeed, *all* of creation—a universal symphony that includes our very own voices—is joined in a celebration of God, and the promise and faith that a holy justice and true equity will triumph over our troubled earth.

PSALM 99

Just as we utter the word *all* seven times in Ps 96 to honor the Presence of God throughout the world, so now, in Ps 99, we utter the name of God itself seven times. For Ps 99 is like a call-and-response coronation hymn: the Holy One is ascending to the universal throne; the Shekhinah, the Sabbath Queen, is arriving.

"Let all praise Your awesome name!" sings the prayer leader, as the community responds, *Kadosh hu!* God is Holy! In fact, the root letters of the Hebrew word for "'holiness"—*k-d-sh* appear and reappear throughout the psalm, for the very heart of the psalm is a celebration of the triumph of holiness in the world—the triumph of justice, fairness, order, and righteousness over the terrifying forces of chaos.

The opening of the psalm seeks to overwhelm us, to awe us: truly to allow oneself to experience the ineffable power and majesty of *Adonai* is to be as shaken to one's core as the psalm describes the land itself being shaken: *Kadosh hu!* God is Holy! Yet this same force —beyond all comprehension in its strength and majesty—is *also* revealed to us through justice, equity, order. That seems to me a wondrous and profoundly humbling notion, for it tells us that justice and true righteousness are *divinely* ordained. Taking action toward making the world a place of justice becomes our responsibility to God. Finally, just as God held those who transgressed to account but also forgave our ancestors so, too, the psalm tells us, God is revealed to us through acts of forgiveness—for "God is holy!"

The psalm calls to us to bow to "God's Holy Mountain," to Zion. Perhaps if we did lower our heads as we say those words, we could, if only for a miraculous moment, experience the ineffable holiness of our God.

PSALM 29

With an exuberant explosiveness and pulsating energy, the Sovereign—whose reign in the universe we have celebrated in the previous psalms—bursts forth now in great and thunderous images, the very climax of the *Kabbalat Shabbat* psalms. Like the angels we echo in the Kedushah—

Kadosh! Kadosh! Adonai of hosts, the whole earth is filled with God's glory!—the psalm here, too, conjures up the angelic awe of God's glory, as it imagines the overwhelming force of a storm resounding in our ears, flaming across the sky, felling trees, uprooting mountains, and above all, shattering normal consciousness with its energy and power. For at this moment, it is the voice of God we are hearing.

Listen: over and over again, the psalm sings of *kavod*, the glorious reign of God; over and over again, it calls up *kol Adonai*, the voice of *Adonai*, controlling the world of nature, evoking the very story of creation; and over and over again—eighteen times in all!—it acclaims God's name. So powerful is this evocation of the Divine Presence that one of the most important of the Kabbalists in the mountains of Safed in Israel, Isaac Luria, thought this psalm alone was enough to precede *L'kha Dodi*.

Listen again: after the mind-shattering litany of images comes a mind-shattering quiet, a stillness, a sense of peace—the peace that surpasses any we have previously known, one that embraces wholeness and holiness. God ascends the throne; the people are flooded with well-being, and our souls are readied at last for the entry of the beloved companion of *Adonai*, the Shekhinah, the Shabbat. A few moments of quiet as we catch our breath and begin to sing *L'kha Dodi*.

PSALM 95

לְכוּ נְרַנְּנָה לַיהוָה נָרִיעָה לְצוּר יִשְׁעֵנוּ: 1

נְקַדְּמָה פָנָיו בְּתוֹדָה בִּזְמִרוֹת נָרִיעַ לוֹ:

כִּי אֵל גָּדוֹל יְהוָה וּמֶלֶךְ גָּדוֹל עַל־כָּל־אֱלֹהִים:

אֲשֶׁר בְּיָדוֹ מֶחְקְרֵי־אָרֶץ וְתוֹעֲפוֹת הָרִים לוֹ:

אֲשֶׁר־לוֹ הַיָּם וְהוּא עָשָׂהוּ וְיַבֶּשֶׁת יָדָיו יָצָרוּ: 5

בֹּאוּ נִשְׁתַּחֲוֶה וְנִכְרָעָה נִבְרְכָה לִפְנֵי־יְהוָה עֹשֵׂנוּ:

כִּי הוּא אֱלֹהֵינוּ וַאֲנַחְנוּ עַם מַרְעִיתוֹ וְצֹאן יָדוֹ הַיּוֹם

אִם־בְּקֹלוֹ תִשְׁמָעוּ:

אַל־תַּקְשׁוּ לְבַבְכֶם כִּמְרִיבָה כְּיוֹם מַסָּה בַּמִּדְבָּר:

אֲשֶׁר נִסּוּנִי אֲבוֹתֵיכֶם בְּחָנוּנִי גַּם־רָאוּ פָעֳלִי:

אַרְבָּעִים שָׁנָה אָקוּט בְּדוֹר וָאֹמַר עַם תֹּעֵי לֵבָב הֵם וְהֵם 10

לֹא־יָדְעוּ דְרָכָי:

אֲשֶׁר־נִשְׁבַּעְתִּי בְאַפִּי אִם־יְבֹאוּן אֶל־מְנוּחָתִי:

PSALM 95

1 Come, let us sing with joy to *Adonai*—
   calling out to the Rock who protects us,
let us move closer to God's Presence with gratitude
and in our psalms sing joyously to God!
For *Adonai* is great, Ruler of all other rulers:
the depths of the earth are in God's hands
   the peaks of the mountains are God's.

5 The sea is God's, for God made it; the hands of God formed
   dry land.

So come, let us worship, kneel, bow before *Adonai* our
   Maker:
This is our God and we are
the people of God's pasture,
   the flock in God's hand

   if only we finally heed God's Voice:

*Oh do not harden your hearts as you did at Merivah, as you
   did at Massah
   in the desert wilderness when your ancestors tried and
   tested Me
though they had seen My marvelous acts.*

10 *All forty years I strove with that generation till
I said, "These people have errant hearts. They will never
   honor My Ways."
And I swore in My rage that never
would they come
to My place of rest.*

PSALM 96

1 שִׁירוּ לַיהוָה שִׁיר חָדָשׁ שִׁירוּ לַיהוָה כָּל־הָאָרֶץ:

שִׁירוּ לַיהוָה בָּרְכוּ שְׁמוֹ בַּשְּׂרוּ מִיּוֹם־לְיוֹם יְשׁוּעָתוֹ:

סַפְּרוּ בַגּוֹיִם כְּבוֹדוֹ בְּכָל־הָעַמִּים נִפְלְאוֹתָיו:

כִּי גָדוֹל יְהוָה וּמְהֻלָּל מְאֹד נוֹרָא הוּא עַל־כָּל־אֱלֹהִים:

5 כִּי כָּל־אֱלֹהֵי הָעַמִּים אֱלִילִים וַיהוָה שָׁמַיִם עָשָׂה:

הוֹד־וְהָדָר לְפָנָיו עֹז וְתִפְאֶרֶת בְּמִקְדָּשׁוֹ:

הָבוּ לַיהוָה מִשְׁפְּחוֹת עַמִּים הָבוּ לַיהוָה כָּבוֹד וָעֹז:

הָבוּ לַיהוָה כְּבוֹד שְׁמוֹ שְׂאוּ־מִנְחָה וּבֹאוּ לְחַצְרוֹתָיו:

הִשְׁתַּחֲווּ לַיהוָה בְּהַדְרַת־קֹדֶשׁ חִילוּ מִפָּנָיו כָּל־הָאָרֶץ:

10 אִמְרוּ בַגּוֹיִם יְהוָה מָלָךְ אַף־תִּכּוֹן תֵּבֵל בַּל־תִּמּוֹט יָדִין

עַמִּים בְּמֵישָׁרִים:

יִשְׂמְחוּ הַשָּׁמַיִם וְתָגֵל הָאָרֶץ יִרְעַם הַיָּם וּמְלֹאוֹ:

יַעֲלֹז שָׂדַי וְכָל־אֲשֶׁר־בּוֹ אָז יְרַנְּנוּ כָּל־עֲצֵי־יָעַר:

לִפְנֵי יְהוָה כִּי בָא כִּי בָא לִשְׁפֹּט הָאָרֶץ יִשְׁפֹּט־תֵּבֵל בְּצֶדֶק

וְעַמִּים בֶּאֱמוּנָתוֹ:

PSALM 96

1 Sing a new song to *Adonai!* All the earth, sing to *Adonai!*
Sing to *Adonai,* bless God's Name, spread word of God's
help day after day!
Tell all the nations of God's glory, tell all the people of God's
wondrous acts!
For great is *Adonai,* worthy of praise, more awe-inspiring
than all other gods

5 Other kinds of gods are mere idols, but *Adonai* brought the
heavens into being:
O, the radiance of God glows in the sky; strength, beauty,
are God's holy place.
To *Adonai,* family of nations, to *Adonai,* grant glorious
strength!
Grant to *Adonai* the glory due the Name, bring an offering,
come to God's court:
Worship *Adonai* in sacred space, tremble before God, all
the earth!

10 Let all the nations know *Adonai* rules: the world stands firm
and will not falter, for God judges all peoples fairly.

O heavens rejoice! earth, exult! let the sea and its fullness
roar!
Let the field be glad—and all that is in it, all the trees in the
forest
shout with joy!
For *Adonai* is coming, *Adonai* is on the way,
to judge the land,
to judge the earth
with true justice,
and the peoples of the world with truth.

PSALM 97

1   יְהוָֹה מָלָךְ תָּגֵל הָאָרֶץ יִשְׂמְחוּ אִיִּים רַבִּים:

עָנָן וַעֲרָפֶל סְבִיבָיו צֶדֶק וּמִשְׁפָּט מְכוֹן כִּסְאוֹ:

אֵשׁ לְפָנָיו תֵּלֵךְ וּתְלַהֵט סָבִיב צָרָיו:

הֵאִירוּ בְרָקָיו תֵּבֵל רָאֲתָה וַתָּחֵל הָאָרֶץ:

5   הָרִים כַּדּוֹנַג נָמַסּוּ מִלִּפְנֵי יְהוָֹה מִלִּפְנֵי אֲדוֹן כָּל־הָאָרֶץ:

הִגִּידוּ הַשָּׁמַיִם צִדְקוֹ וְרָאוּ כָל־הָעַמִּים כְּבוֹדוֹ:

יֵבֹשׁוּ כָּל־עֹבְדֵי פֶסֶל הַמִּתְהַלְלִים בָּאֱלִילִים

הִשְׁתַּחֲווּ־לוֹ כָּל־אֱלֹהִים:

שָׁמְעָה וַתִּשְׂמַח צִיּוֹן וַתָּגֵלְנָה בְּנוֹת יְהוּדָה

לְמַעַן מִשְׁפָּטֶיךָ יְהוָֹה:

כִּי־אַתָּה יְהוָֹה עֶלְיוֹן עַל־כָּל־הָאָרֶץ מְאֹד נַעֲלֵיתָ

עַל־כָּל־אֱלֹהִים:

10   אֹהֲבֵי יְהוָֹה שִׂנְאוּ רָע שֹׁמֵר נַפְשׁוֹת חֲסִידָיו

מִיַּד רְשָׁעִים יַצִּילֵם:

אוֹר זָרֻעַ לַצַּדִּיק וּלְיִשְׁרֵי־לֵב שִׂמְחָה:

שִׂמְחוּ צַדִּיקִים בַּיהוָֹה וְהוֹדוּ לְזֵכֶר קָדְשׁוֹ:

PSALM 97

1   *Adonai* reigns! Let the earth rejoice, let islands exult!
    Dark clouds surround God,
       but law and justice are the base of God's throne—
    Fire heralds God's Presence—and the adversaries
    around God burn.
    God's bolts of lightning light up the world—
    the world sees—
    the earth trembles—

5   as if they were wax, mountains melt—
          before *Adonai,* before the God
          of the whole world.

    The heavens proclaim God's justice—
    All the peoples of the world see God's glory,
    Shamed are all worshipers of worthless images,
    all kneel to God on their knees.
    How Zion hears and rejoices!
    How the towns of Judah exult
    because of your judgments, O *Adonai!* Because it is You
    supreme in the world, You
    Who surpass any other gods.—

10 Lovers of *Adonai,* shun evil — and God will protect you
    from the hands of the wicked.
    God will save you.
    Light is sown for the just,
    and for those with an honest heart,
         there is joy
    Rejoice, O just ones, in *Adonai,*
    praise God's holy Name.

PSALM 98

1 מִזְמוֹר שִׁירוּ לַיהֹוָה שִׁיר חָדָשׁ כִּי־נִפְלָאוֹת עָשָׂה הוֹשִׁיעָה־לּוֹ
יְמִינוֹ וּזְרוֹעַ קָדְשׁוֹ:

הוֹדִיעַ יְהֹוָה יְשׁוּעָתוֹ לְעֵינֵי הַגּוֹיִם גִּלָּה צִדְקָתוֹ:

זָכַר חַסְדּוֹ וֶאֱמוּנָתוֹ לְבֵית יִשְׂרָאֵל רָאוּ כָל־אַפְסֵי־אָרֶץ אֵת
יְשׁוּעַת אֱלֹהֵינוּ:

הָרִיעוּ לַיהֹוָה כָּל־הָאָרֶץ פִּצְחוּ וְרַנְּנוּ וְזַמֵּרוּ:

5 זַמְּרוּ לַיהֹוָה בְּכִנּוֹר בְּכִנּוֹר וְקוֹל זִמְרָה:

בַּחֲצֹצְרוֹת וְקוֹל שׁוֹפָר הָרִיעוּ לִפְנֵי הַמֶּלֶךְ יְהֹוָה:

יִרְעַם הַיָּם וּמְלֹאוֹ תֵּבֵל וְיֹשְׁבֵי בָהּ:

נְהָרוֹת יִמְחֲאוּ־כָף יַחַד הָרִים יְרַנֵּנוּ:

לִפְנֵי־יְהֹוָה כִּי בָא לִשְׁפֹּט הָאָרֶץ יִשְׁפֹּט־תֵּבֵל בְּצֶדֶק
וְעַמִּים בְּמֵישָׁרִים:

PSALM 98

1 Sing a new song to *Adonai* Who has worked wonders,
   Whose right hand and holy arm have triumphed!
   Adonai has revealed a saving power:
   victory in the eyes of the world,
   sturdy kindness and loyalty to Israel.

   The very ends of the earth saw
   the saving power
   of our God.

   O, make a joyful noise to *Adonai* all the earth,
   Burst into songs and praise!
   Shout out, sing out,
       make music!

5 Play music for *Adonai* on the lyres—
   With lyres—and the sound of music!
   With trumpets and the call of the shofar
   raise a shout to our Sovereign *Adonai!*

   Let the sea and all its fullness roar!
   The world and all dwelling here!
   Let rivers clap their hands—let mountains shout with joy
   before *Adonai* who is coming
       Who is coming
   to judge the earth
   justly
   and with equity, the peoples
   of the world.

PSALM 99

1 יְהֹוָה מָלָךְ יִרְגְּזוּ עַמִּים יֹשֵׁב כְּרוּבִים תָּנוּט הָאָרֶץ:

יְהֹוָה בְּצִיּוֹן גָּדוֹל וְרָם הוּא עַל־כָּל־הָעַמִּים:

יוֹדוּ שִׁמְךָ גָּדוֹל וְנוֹרָא קָדוֹשׁ הוּא:

וְעֹז מֶלֶךְ מִשְׁפָּט אָהֵב אַתָּה כּוֹנַנְתָּ מֵישָׁרִים מִשְׁפָּט וּצְדָקָה

בְּיַעֲקֹב אַתָּה עָשִׂיתָ:

5 רוֹמְמוּ יְהֹוָה אֱלֹהֵינוּ וְהִשְׁתַּחֲווּ לַהֲדֹם רַגְלָיו קָדוֹשׁ הוּא:

מֹשֶׁה וְאַהֲרֹן בְּכֹהֲנָיו וּשְׁמוּאֵל בְּקֹרְאֵי שְׁמוֹ קֹרִאים אֶל־יְהֹוָה

וְהוּא יַעֲנֵם:

בְּעַמּוּד עָנָן יְדַבֵּר אֲלֵיהֶם שָׁמְרוּ עֵדֹתָיו וְחֹק נָתַן־לָמוֹ:

יְהֹוָה אֱלֹהֵינוּ אַתָּה עֲנִיתָם אֵל נֹשֵׂא הָיִיתָ לָהֶם וְנֹקֵם

עַל־עֲלִילוֹתָם:

רוֹמְמוּ יְהֹוָה אֱלֹהֵינוּ וְהִשְׁתַּחֲווּ לְהַר קָדְשׁוֹ כִּי־קָדוֹשׁ

יְהֹוָה אֱלֹהֵינוּ:

PSALM 99

1 *Adonai* reigns! Before God's throne
nations tremble — the land quakes!
Adonai is great in Zion—
    celebrated by the nations of the world:
All praise Your wondrous Name:
    God is Holy!

With the strength of a Sovereign who loves justice, You
established order
and brought true judgment to Jacob.

5 Praise *Adonai* our God,
    bow before God's footstool:
    God is Holy!

Moshe,
the priest Aharon
and Shmu'el, among the God-seekers
called to *Adonai*
and *Adonai* answered them:

In a pillar of cloud, God spoke to them—
they honored God's Torah, they kept God's laws.

You answered them, *Adonai,* our God.
You were a forgiving God though You punished
    wrongdoing.

O praise *Adonai* our God, bow before God's
    holy mountain,
For *Adonai* our God is
    holy!

PSALM 29

1   מִזְמוֹר לְדָוִד הָבוּ לַיהוָה בְּנֵי אֵלִים הָבוּ לַיהוָה כָּבוֹד וָעֹז:

הָבוּ לַיהוָה כְּבוֹד שְׁמוֹ הִשְׁתַּחֲווּ לַיהוָה בְּהַדְרַת־קֹדֶשׁ:

קוֹל יְהוָה עַל־הַמָּיִם אֵל־הַכָּבוֹד הִרְעִים יְהוָה עַל־מַיִם רַבִּים:

קוֹל־יְהוָה בַּכֹּחַ קוֹל יְהוָה בֶּהָדָר:

5   קוֹל יְהוָה שֹׁבֵר אֲרָזִים וַיְשַׁבֵּר יְהוָה אֶת־אַרְזֵי הַלְּבָנוֹן:

וַיַּרְקִידֵם כְּמוֹ־עֵגֶל לְבָנוֹן וְשִׂרְיֹן כְּמוֹ בֶן־רְאֵמִים:

קוֹל־יְהוָה חֹצֵב לַהֲבוֹת אֵשׁ:

קוֹל יְהוָה יָחִיל מִדְבָּר יָחִיל יְהוָה מִדְבַּר קָדֵשׁ:

קוֹל יְהוָה יְחוֹלֵל אַיָּלוֹת וַיֶּחֱשֹׂף יְעָרוֹת וּבְהֵיכָלוֹ

כֻּלּוֹ אֹמֵר כָּבוֹד:

10   יְהוָה לַמַּבּוּל יָשָׁב וַיֵּשֶׁב יְהוָה מֶלֶךְ לְעוֹלָם:

יְהוָה עֹז לְעַמּוֹ יִתֵּן יְהוָה יְבָרֵךְ אֶת־עַמּוֹ בַשָּׁלוֹם:

PSALM 29

1 *A Psalm of David.*
  Ascribe to *Adonai*, oh divine beings, ascribe to *Adonai*
      glorious strength!
  Ascribe to *Adonai* the glory due God's Name, worship
      Adonai in the
      beauty of holiness!

  The voice of *Adonai* roars on the water! The God of glory
      thunders,
      Adonai thundering over the great seas!
  The voice of *Adonai* is filled with power, the voice of
      Adonai
      majestic:

5 The voice of *Adonai* shatters the cedars, *Adonai* shatters into
      pieces
      the cedars of Lebanon—
  making Lebanon skip like a calf, Mount Hermon like a wild
      young ox:

  The voice of *Adonai* hews out lightning, flaming, like fire:
  The voice of *Adonai* shakes the desert—
  the wilderness of Kadesh *Adonai* makes tremble:
  The voice of *Adonai* swirls through the oaks
  strips the forests bare
      as in the palace of God
      all call "Glory!"

10 *Adonai* reigned over the Flood, *Adonai* will reign for all time
   May *Adonai* give strength to God's people,
   May *Adonai* bless the people with peace.

CHAPTER TEN

Starry Heavens, Moral Law:

Shabbat Morning's "Verses of Song"

On Shabbat mornings, I seem to be one of those oddballs (at least at my shul!) for whom being in my *makom kavua*, my usual seat, in time for the preliminary service called *Pesukei Dezimra* is very, very important. As our congregation begins reciting the nine psalms that precede the *Ashrei*, I usually go into my own prayer-world, where one of the psalms jumps off the page at me, asking for my attention. I begin reciting each line of the psalm consciously and slowly. I pause when my attention is riveted by a particular phrase, a particular image—"tall as a cedar in Lebanon," perhaps; "*Adonai* is close to all those whose hearts are broken . . ." "Who understands why we stumble?" . . . "May we ourselves feel Your loveliness, *Adonai*, our God. . . ."

I feel as if I am befriending the psalm anew.

That kind of quiet, meditative exercise serves as a way of readying myself for the prayers of the Morning Service—I put aside whatever was on my mind before I walked into the synagogue and enter the mind-set of prayer.

But to savor these psalms, you don't have to be in synagogue on Shabbat morning—nor must reciting the psalms be limited only to Shabbat. Not all of them may speak to you all of the time, and one or two may *never* speak to you—Pss 135 and 136, for example, are psalms meant for public declaration rather than private contemplation, more liturgical ritual than poem-prayer.

But so many of the Shabbat morning psalms are so spiritually, emotionally, and psychologically evocative, or at the least possess individual lines that are evocative, that they cry out for our attention. And by giving them our attention, we are truly renewed.

The psalms included in the *Pesukei Dezimra* of Shabbat morning touch upon such a wide range of themes and on so many areas of our lives. They offer us an ecstatic appreciation of the world God has made and the pervasive sense that this *is* indeed a God-infused world that we live in. They poignantly insist on how fleeting life is, expressing the longing to make the short time we have here meaningful. They acknowledge with humility our vulnerability to sin, whether unwittingly or intentionally. They express faith that when our hearts are broken, our souls are troubled, and our spirits are crushed, *Adonai* is there to receive our entreaties, to offer protective shelter. And, at last, the psalms are alive with a true love of Torah and a conviction that God's Torah can transform our lives.

No summary of the themes of the opening psalms can convey the richness and power of the process of *praying* them. The words and images of the psalms come alive only in the process of getting to know them, by coming into relationship with them, by allowing yourself to feel them. The process is unique for each of us. For example, what is conjured up in a sculptor's soul by the line

> *may the works of our own hands be realized, the works of our own hands realized*

has a different resonance from what is conjured up in the soul of a scientist, a mother, a baker, an architect, a writer, a dreamer.

I invite you to savor these psalms, one by one— perhaps one each day, or even one each week. In the words of the psalmist:

> "O fill yourselves with awe for *Adonai*, you holy ones, and never again shall you feel lack." (Ps 34)

PSALM 19

The philosopher Kant once said he was moved to believe in God by studying "the starry heavens and the moral law." I don't think there is a psalm that more exquisitely exemplifies the beauty of both "the starry heavens" and "the moral law" than Ps 19, which opens *Pesukei Dezimra* on Shabbat morning. Lambent and luminous, the psalm, like a slowly moving shaft of sunlight, celebrates one by one the beauty and power of nature and its rhythms; the profoundly rich and transformative gift of Torah, and finally, the struggles and journey of one's inner world, as if we, too, are longing to shine. All the core themes and patterns of the Morning Service are here in microcosm: the celebration of the "new light" that will shine in Zion; God as the Creator of light; Torah; the Shema, and God as savior of Israel .

Here Comes the Sun

The psalm begins with a description of the sky so stirring that its song evokes the ancient image of "the music of the spheres," the heavenly harmonics of the planets, the stars, the galaxies—all an expression of "God's glory," which is what the brilliantly sophisticated philosopher Immanuel Kant himself felt. Amidst the splendor of God's sky—"like a groom striding from his marriage canopy"—proudly, heroically, the sun comes out.

Is your first reaction to rush for the sunblock?

So fearful of the power of the sun have we Americans become, that we have lost our capacity to celebrate its glory. So as we plaster on glops of sunblock, why don't we pause for a moment to cherish the sun's beauty and its manifold gifts—gifts that make our whole lives possible? Why not give ourselves a chance to mull over, to meditate on, consciously to experience, the glory of nature's light?

In all honesty, I don't think I myself ever did until one midsummer several years ago when my sister Alyne and I went hiking in northern Finland, above the Arctic Circle. We were in the storied "Land of the Midnight Sun" I had heard about ever since geography class in elementary school. The Land of the Midnight Sun, though, is also the land of long dark winters, and our guide shared with us what it was like to live with darkness for many months of the year. He called it "dream-time," a time to slow down, stay inside, keep warm. Now that it was summer, the excitement and joy all around us was palpable—everywhere we looked, in open fields, people were soaking up the radiance of the sun— even at nine or ten at night. It was as if life itself was restored.

Similarly, journalist Elisabeth Rosenthal describes the excitement buzzing in the town of Longyearbyen, Norway—just six hundred miles from the North Pole—when, after months of living in the perpetual darkness of winter, two young scientists working on the ice first saw "a sliver of sunlight peek around a mountain" in early March:

> As they worked, the shaft of light grew to fill a large swath of the valley. On their way home, they made a beeline with their snowmobiles for the light. And there it was, between two mountains: the sun.
>
> "Look at it!" they shouted in unison. "Look at it!" The scientists hugged, did little jigs in the snow, and then stood motionless, awe-struck.[16]

For the psalm, taking joy in the beauty of the sun as evidence of God's presence in the universe is just the beginning. Even stronger than the light of the sun, for the psalmist, are the sources of *spiritual light* in our lives: the moral law and mitzvot of Torah. The images pour out, identifying how the qualities of Torah are sources of physical, emotional, intellectual, and spiritual transformation: *restoring the spirit; making the simple, wise;*

---

[16]Elisabeth Rosenthal, "A Speck of Sunlight is a Town's Yearly Alarm Clock," *New York Times*, March 3, 2008, A4.

gladdening the heart; filling eyes with light; and ultimately tasting *sweeter than honey dripping from the honeycomb.* How? Why?

Torah, for the psalmist—and for us—is more than a scroll, more than a collection of books—it is a pathway to be followed in life. To speak of Torah is to include the values one lives by, the honoring of mitzvot, the quality of one's relationships with others, one's actions in the daily world. Praying the psalm, we are drawn into pondering whether and when we really did have an experience in which acting in accord with Torah restored a flagging spirit . . . when it brought acceptance where there was grief; joy where there was sorrow. My own associations with that image includes that quiet, modest, sense of comfort—of "restoration of spirit"—that comes when we offer the Prayer for Healing (*Mi Sheberakh*) during the service and the sense of communal peace that fills the congregation. Or the sense of community and connectedness I feel performing the mitzvah of bringing food to a house of mourning . . . Can you identify experiences in which you felt your spirit restored?

And what about *gladdening your heart? filling your eyes with light?* For me, for example, my husband Anthony's sharing with me special moments of his day with residents at the Jewish Home for the Aging, where he is rabbi, affects me in that way; so does baking ḥallah with my daughter Avigail, or studying a challenging passage in Talmud with my *ḥavruta* partners Miriam and Marshall—all these are "sweeter than honey dripping from the honeycomb." What are the moments "sweeter than honey dripping from the honeycomb" in your Jewish life?

The gifts of this psalm continue. In the previous stanza, the mention of *Adonai* was repeated seven times—in the psalms, very much a symbol of wholeness. Now, using another often-appearing number in our tradition (the four children, four cups of wine, and four questions of the Passover seder, for example), the psalmist identifies four kinds of sins. In a kind of psychology of our own souls, the psalmist names those we commit inadvertently when we "stumble"; those we keep hidden from others; those that result from our own arrogance; and finally, the serious transgressions of which we may be guilty. Clearly, if we recite these lines slowly and honestly to ourselves, pausing between each line, reviewing our own lives, the psalm gives us a chance for a significant *heshbon nefesh*, an accounting of our own souls. And it moves from the enumeration of kinds of sins to an extraordinary but gentle and humble appeal, using words that are used elsewhere only in relation to sacrifices, as if this, too, is a way of coming into intimate relationship with God:

> *May the words of my mouth and the meditations of my heart, fulfill Your will,* Adonai, *my Rock and my Redeemer.*

Pausing and speaking that final word, "my Redeemer" slowly, truly taking it in, is emotionally redemptive. At the very end, God's beautiful universe, God's glorious Torah, and our own acknowledged moral and spiritual life are brought together on our very own lips.

PSALM 34

As King Saul madly and relentlessly pursues David in order to kill him, David flees—landing, at one point, with King Akhish (not, actually Avimeleh) of Gat. But his reputation as a fierce warrior follows him, and frightened that Akhish will not protect him, he feigns madness until the king sends him away. He hides out—and is soon joined by "Everyone who was in straits and everyone who was in debt and everyone who was desperate" (1 Sam 22:2). The words that pour out of our psalm are, for the psalmist, words that aptly express what David must have felt in that harrowing time: the sense of desperation, the feeling of wild relief at escaping both Saul and Akhish, the awareness of vulnerability, the vital importance of finding a way of life that would help him feel close to, and protected by, God.

But the most extraordinary moment of the psalm—and the one, I think, that can be most challenging for us today—is the joyous exclamation: *O taste and see that* Adonai *is good!"*

What does it mean to "taste" God?

Not surprisingly, our traditional commentators are not wholly comfortable with the image: for them, "taste" is understood as "apprehend," in other words, "taste" becomes intellectual knowledge. In some prayer books, indeed, the translation of the line becomes "O consider and see. . . ." But let's not be so ready to flee to our comfort zone, where God-language, God-experience, our whole relationship to God, can be abstracted, intellectualized only. *Fill yourselves with awe for* Adonai, the psalm tells us—another strongly physical, palpable, image. Even more: the psalm contrasts the good of seeking *Adonai* to the hunger suffered by young lions. Their bellies are empty—but ours, in the very act of seeking God, are full.

Because our tradition is so richly intellectual, many of us may tend to disregard all of its soul-pleasing sensory aspects. So much of Jewish life is about community—the warmth of gathering together to pray, to celebrate, to share meals. Wine and ḥallah are fundamental to our religious practice. We take in the aroma of fragrant spices in the act of saying farewell to the Sabbath. We wave our palm frond—the *lulav*—and the exquisitely fragrant *etrog*, the citron—as we march around the synagogue on the harvest festival of Sukkot, when we also take our meals in our royally decorated outdoor booths whose roofs are palm fronds, too. We light olive oil or candles for eight days for Hanukkah; fill our homes with branches of green leaves and our synagogues with roses for Shavuot.

At its core, too, Judaism is an *embodied* faith: it is what we *do*—even more than what we believe—that counts. The Torah doesn't tell us what we must believe, what we must think; it tells us what mitzvot we must perform in order to honor God in our lives. One could even argue that it is only through actually honoring the commandments that we come to discover what we actually believe.

In this context, "to taste and see that *Adonai* is good," is an invitation to engage all of our senses as human beings, the whole of our God-given body, in the experience of sacred living. How do we do that? The psalms suggests to us that if we are alive to the tastes and smells and sounds and touch of the world we live in and alive to the tastes and smells and sounds and touch of our own tradition, we will be drawn to "avoid evil and do good." In the end, the more viscerally we experience the deep pleasure of being alive, here, and created in the image of God, the more we will "seek peace and pursue it."

Bete'avon.

PSALM 90

If we were reading the psalms according to their order in the book of Psalms, we would have come to Ps 90 after reading Ps 89, which ends Book Three of the Psalms in anguished mourning. The psalm laments the loss of David's monarchy: "How long, *Adonai*, will You hide Your face? How long will Your fury blaze like fire?" that psalm asks, crying out that although God had promised that David's line would be established "as long as the heavens last," God has "rejected, spurned, and become at enraged" him. Opening Book Four, Ps 90 comes to assure us that, though David's monarchy has been destroyed, not everything has been destroyed: despite the terrible losses of the past, God has nevertheless still remained our refuge "generation after generation." In that sense, this is a recuperative psalm, depicting with a kind of straightforward tenderness and sense of vulnerability, the reality of time itself: the melancholy reality of the brevity and challenges of human life—so distinct from the eternality of the Holy One. Perhaps it is this simple truth-telling, this acknowledgment of the fundamental issues of life, that makes this psalm a healing one and is one reason that it is read not only here, in *Pesukei D'zimra*, but also, indeed, at funerals.

The most resonant line of the psalm for many of us—for me, the one that sends out ripples of thought and feeling every time I pray it—is:

> *Adonai*, teach us how to make each of our days matter
> so that our hearts may become wise.

A story. My husband Anthony and I met and fell in love during my third year of rabbinic studies in Jerusalem—I was already in my late fifties, and Anthony had hit sixty. At our wedding that fall in Los Angeles, Rabbi Ed Feinstein spoke of, on the one hand, our courage in making this commitment to one another at this stage of life, and on the other, the vital importance of our realizing that what we have—and indeed, what all of us have—is actually only *hayom*. All we have is Today. Rabbi Feinstein's message at our wedding has shaped our whole marriage: knowing that this is all we have; we have tried never taking one another for granted, not letting one day go by without expressing how much we cherish one another and how grateful we are to have found one another, nor have we let disagreements linger.

Though they may sound similar, the call to cherish *hayom* is not the same as the notion of *carpe diem*, "seize the day"—in a way, really, they are actually opposites. The idea of "seizing the day" has, as its assumption, that tomorrow doesn't matter, and so you need not worry about the ethical or moral or physical consequences of any action you take today. "Seizing the day" is like exploiting the day: there's oil in those fields, grab it now; there's money to be made, go for it; there's a lottery ticket, buy it now. The positive side of "seizing the day" is that it can encourage people who are hemmed in by fears to let go and take a risk. The negative side is that in taking advantage of immediate possibilities, you ignore the consequences and outcomes of your actions.

But cherishing *hayom*, cherishing today, is not about "seizing" anything. It is about not procrastinating, not putting off expressions of caring, love, goodness, truth, right action. It is recognizing that, if there is a tomorrow, it will be based on what we say, the way we live, the choices we make, the actions we perform, today. If, rather than act blindly or say whatever we feel like when we feel like it and regardless of the hurt we may cause others; we pay attention to what we are doing, we allow ourselves to be fully present with all of our faculties now and here; then we have a chance of learning about the effects of our emotion, expression, thought, actions. We have a chance to grow. We have a chance to come into authentic relationship with others. And that, I think, is what the psalmist means by becoming "wise."

What I have learned from this psalm and from Rabbi Feinstein, is it is worth a try.

PSALM 91

Do we believe—can we believe—the theology of psalm 91? Is God a vast mother bird who will shelter us under her wings? If we call upon God, and cling to God, is there really any chance of our being guaranteed a long life? Why then do the innocent suffer? Why then do loving, God-believing children die?

Psalm 91 is most deeply felt, appreciated, and grasped when it is *not* regarded as a series of statements about an objective truth. Rather, the psalm, is like a mandala, or, as Israeli scholar Yair Hoffman has suggested, an "amulet."[17] It is through our very praying of the psalm, our chanting of it, that our own experience of God's protective care of us can be felt and that feeling strengthened. It is one of the psalms for which the process of Holy Reading can be most powerful.

To repeat a line that evokes the ways in which God will protect us, to rest with that line, to ponder it, is to begin to become open to feel it and internalize it deeply. Our souls are comforted. Most remarkably, we discover that it is *the spiritual energy gener-*

[17]See Alter, *The Book of Psalms*, p. 321 n1.

ated by our recitation of the psalm that is itself vividly captured by
the image of the angels who lift us up by their psalms. That spiritual energy intensified by our expression of faith *is* the angel that
will be there for us . . . the angel of our own spiritual self
enriched, enhanced, by our connection with God.

PSALMS 135 and 136

The first two psalms that follow Ps 91 in the Shabbat morning
Pesukei Dezimra differ greatly from those that have come before.
Whereas the previous psalms are personal prayers, psalms enriched
by individual engagement with their often moving, sometimes
provocative, images and ideas, Pss 135 and 136 are intended for
public recitation, aloud. Martin S. Cohen offers a vivid description
of the ancient mise-en-scene in the Temple:

> The Levites are in position on their risers. The priests are in place
> with the livestock in the innermost courtyard. The public is gath-
> ered in the other Temple courtyards . . . The song leader calls out
> for hymns of praise from all those standing in the Temple courts:
> they are to demonstrate their participation in the sacrificial ser-
> vice by chanting hymns of praise to God while the priests actually
> perform the animal sacrifices . . . All are to join in. . . .

As for Ps 136, says Cohen,

> one can imagine the clarion voice of, say, an especially gifted
> Levitical tenor singing out the first half of each line while the citi-
> zenry, crammed into the Temple courtyards and led by the Leviti-
> cal choir in place on their performance platform, responded in
> joyous response that, yes, divine mercy really is forever.[18]

The psalms heroically depict *Adonai* in ways we have
encountered earlier. *Adonai* is the God of nature, Controller of
the winds and the rain, Creator of the world, as well as the God
of history, treasuring the people Israel, liberating them from

---

[18]Martin S. Cohen, *Our Haven and our Strength: The Book of Psalms* (New York:
Aviv Press, 2004), pp. 433–36.

slavery in Egypt, conquering the Egyptian oppressors, and finally, bringing the Israelites into Canaan, after defeating the armies of kings Siḥon and Og who would not let the Israelites pass through their territories. The psalms are almost like national anthems: songs of heroism and triumph, celebrating God and the nation, while dismissing the lesser gods of silver and gold made by human hands.

Taken together, the two psalms present us with a spiritual and imaginative challenge. Is the phrase "God's kindness is forever," repeated twenty-six times in Ps 136, just a litany we repeat by rote; or does it, can it, truly have meaning for us today? If we were to take the ancient litany and bring it "up to date"—stretch it from 70 CE, from the day the Temple was destroyed to the twenty-first century—for which events in our history would we want to give thanks to God?

Psalm 136, for which we traditionally rise, is called the Great Hallel, the "Great Song of Praise." Perhaps the most awe-inspiring reality for which we can praise God in a Great Hallel today is the remarkable, inexplicable fact that our people are still here.

PSALM 33

Every time we imagine that we can make a nice, neat, definitive, incontrovertible statement about an aspect of Judaism, a different text comes along to disprove it. Judaism rarely lets us rest on our laurels, close our minds, allow ourselves to become intellectually or spiritually smug. The placement of Ps 33 after Pss 135 and 136 in the *Pesukei Dezimra* typifies this characteristic of our faith.

For even though it was God, not the Israelites, who was praised as Warrior-in-Chief, both Pss 135 and 136 celebrate military victories—over the Egyptians, over the "mighty kings" who stood in the way of Israel's entrance into Canaan. Like the book of Joshua (24:1-14), neither psalm even mentions the Revelation at Sinai; the core events of Israelite history here are the liberation from Egypt and the conquest of Canaan.

But now comes Ps 33 to undo any relish we might take in our status as conquerors, as victors brought into the Promised Land by the military prowess of our God. It is as though the words of the prophet Zekhariah are echoing in the background: ". . . not by might and not by power, but by My spirit, says *Adonai* of Hosts . . ." (Zech 4:7). Similarly, Ps 33 reminds us:

> A ruler is not rescued by a great army,
> a hero is not rescued by great strength —
> a horse cannot save you; its mighty strength
> helps no one escape.

The psalm undoes not only the threat of self-satisfaction in military victory which the previous psalms may have aroused in us; it also undoes any narrow sense of nationalism. For it reminds us that God sees *all* human beings and has fashioned *all* human hearts.

Israel may be God's treasured people, as the previous psalms insisted. But as we come to the end of the nine special psalms of Shabbat's *Pesukei Dezimra* and prepare ourselves for the psalms of praise of the Daily Hallel, Ps 33 seeks to drive home that perhaps even more than God loves Israel does God love "the right and the just." May we merit, by acting justly, that God's kindness "be upon us."

Holy Reading: Psalm 19

So many lines and phrases from the Shabbat morning psalms beckon us to linger upon them, mull them over, draw them into our own hearts, allow them to become infused with our own personal meaning, our own individual experience, our own pleasures and our own pains. That is especially true with Psalm 19. For example, when I recite its opening line— *"The skies declare the glory of God—the heavens, the work of God's hands,"* I often see in my mind's eye images that have profoundly moved me: the soul-stirring photographs from the Hubble telescope, vivid with fiery galaxies swirling millions of light-years away; the fat golden moon of Sukkot over the Negev sands; the magnificent sunsets over the Pacific. I invite you to focus on what *you* see as "the glory of God" in the skies . . . "the work of God's hands. . . ."

Later in the psalm, comes a question that troubled the psalmist as much as it does most of us today: *"Who understands why we stumble?"* And then begins a plea for being "cleansed" from our own troubling secrets, from our own arrogance, from any "great wrongs." If we allow ourselves to pause and take those words seriously, to meditate upon them, we can experience, here and now, in this very moment, a quiet process of *heshbon nefesh*, of making an account of our life. In what ways do I feel as if I'm stumbling? Where have I been arrogant, this last week? What secrets am I keeping about myself, that cause me shame?

On another day, a different image from the psalm might spark our concentration. Perhaps it is the inviting, lush, line: *"The Torah of Adonai is . . . sweeter than honey dripping from the honeycomb."* Letting those words roll around in one's mouth, in Hebrew *or* English, is itself so full of pleasure—a pleasure that grows even richer if we repeat them over and over as at the same time we seek to discover in what specific ways that image is true for *us*. We might even discover, along the way, that by opening ourselves to that pleasure we find ourselves, in the words of the psalm, truly, gloriously, "glowing with Torah."

PSALM 19

1 לַמְנַצֵּחַ מִזְמוֹר לְדָוִד:

הַשָּׁמַיִם מְסַפְּרִים כְּבוֹד־אֵל וּמַעֲשֵׂה יָדָיו מַגִּיד הָרָקִיעַ:

יוֹם לְיוֹם יַבִּיעַ אֹמֶר וְלַיְלָה לְּלַיְלָה יְחַוֶּה־דָּעַת:

אֵין אֹמֶר וְאֵין דְּבָרִים בְּלִי נִשְׁמָע קוֹלָם:

5 בְּכָל־הָאָרֶץ יָצָא קַוָּם וּבִקְצֵה תֵבֵל מִלֵּיהֶם לַשֶּׁמֶשׁ שָׂם
אֹהֶל בָּהֶם:

וְהוּא כְּחָתָן יֹצֵא מֵחֻפָּתוֹ יָשִׂישׂ כְּגִבּוֹר לָרוּץ אֹרַח:

מִקְצֵה הַשָּׁמַיִם מוֹצָאוֹ וּתְקוּפָתוֹ עַל־קְצוֹתָם
וְאֵין נִסְתָּר מֵחַמָּתוֹ:

תּוֹרַת יְהוָה תְּמִימָה מְשִׁיבַת נָפֶשׁ עֵדוּת יְהוָה נֶאֱמָנָה
מַחְכִּימַת פֶּתִי:

פִּקּוּדֵי יְהוָה יְשָׁרִים מְשַׂמְּחֵי־לֵב מִצְוַת יְהוָה
בָּרָה מְאִירַת עֵינָיִם:

10 יִרְאַת יְהוָה טְהוֹרָה עוֹמֶדֶת לָעַד מִשְׁפְּטֵי־יְהוָה אֱמֶת
צָדְקוּ יַחְדָּו:

הַנֶּחֱמָדִים מִזָּהָב וּמִפַּז רָב וּמְתוּקִים מִדְּבַשׁ וְנֹפֶת צוּפִים:

גַּם־עַבְדְּךָ נִזְהָר בָּהֶם בְּשָׁמְרָם עֵקֶב רָב:

שְׁגִיאוֹת מִי־יָבִין מִנִּסְתָּרוֹת נַקֵּנִי:

גַּם מִזֵּדִים חֲשֹׂךְ עַבְדֶּךָ אַל־יִמְשְׁלוּ־בִי אָז אֵיתָם וְנִקֵּיתִי
מִפֶּשַׁע רָב:

15 יִהְיוּ לְרָצוֹן אִמְרֵי־פִי וְהֶגְיוֹן לִבִּי לְפָנֶיךָ יְהוָה צוּרִי וְגֹאֲלִי:

PSALM 19

1   *To the conductor, a David psalm.*
    The skies declare the glory of God—the heavens, the work
        of God's hands.
    Day pours out word of it to day, night to night tells its
        knowledge—
    There is no speech, there are no words, that go unheard:
    The sounds of their praise reach all the world; their words
        reach the ends of the earth.

5   God sets up a tent for the sun in the heavens
    and like a groom striding
    from the marriage canopy,
        it comes out now
    rejoicing, like a hero running his course. The sun comes out
    at the edge of the heavens, making its circuit to the other
        edge,
    warming every corner of the world.

    The Torah of *Adonai* is perfect, restoring the spirit—
    The Torah of *Adonai* is sure, making the simple, wise—
    The Torah of *Adonai* is honest, gladdening the heart—
    The Torah of *Adonai* is clear, filling eyes with light—

10 The Torah of *Adonai* is pure, enduring forever—
    The Torah of *Adonai* is true, and altogether just:
    more desirable than gold, than even the finest gold,
    sweeter than honey dripping from the honeycomb.
    I, too, glow with Torah
    and with the great reward in showing it honor.

    Who understands why we stumble?
    But from the sins I keep secret, please cleanse me—
    save me from my own arrogance—don't let it control me—
    cleanse me of of any great wrongs.

15 *May the words of my mouth, and the meditations of my
        heart, fulfill Your will,*
    Adonai, *my Rock and my Redeemer.*

PSALM 34

1 לְדָוִד בְּשַׁנּוֹתוֹ אֶת־טַעְמוֹ לִפְנֵי אֲבִימֶלֶךְ וַיְגָרְשֵׁהוּ וַיֵּלַךְ:

אֲבָרֲכָה אֶת־יְהוָה בְּכָל־עֵת תָּמִיד תְּהִלָּתוֹ בְּפִי:

בַּיהוָה תִּתְהַלֵּל נַפְשִׁי יִשְׁמְעוּ עֲנָוִים וְיִשְׂמָחוּ:

גַּדְּלוּ לַיהוָה אִתִּי וּנְרוֹמְמָה שְׁמוֹ יַחְדָּו:

5 דָּרַשְׁתִּי אֶת־יְהוָה וְעָנָנִי וּמִכָּל־מְגוּרוֹתַי הִצִּילָנִי:

הִבִּיטוּ אֵלָיו וְנָהָרוּ וּפְנֵיהֶם אַל־יֶחְפָּרוּ:

זֶה עָנִי קָרָא וַיהוָה שָׁמֵעַ וּמִכָּל־צָרוֹתָיו הוֹשִׁיעוֹ:

חֹנֶה מַלְאַךְ־יְהוָה סָבִיב לִירֵאָיו וַיְחַלְּצֵם:

טַעֲמוּ וּרְאוּ כִּי־טוֹב יְהוָה אַשְׁרֵי הַגֶּבֶר יֶחֱסֶה־בּוֹ:

10 יְראוּ אֶת־יְהוָה קְדֹשָׁיו כִּי אֵין מַחְסוֹר לִירֵאָיו:

כְּפִירִים רָשׁוּ וְרָעֵבוּ וְדֹרְשֵׁי יְהוָה לֹא־יַחְסְרוּ כָל־טוֹב:

לְכוּ־בָנִים שִׁמְעוּ־לִי יִרְאַת יְהוָה אֲלַמֶּדְכֶם:

מִי־הָאִישׁ הֶחָפֵץ חַיִּים אֹהֵב יָמִים לִרְאוֹת טוֹב:

נְצֹר לְשׁוֹנְךָ מֵרָע וּשְׂפָתֶיךָ מִדַּבֵּר מִרְמָה:

PSALM 34

1 *A David Psalm, when he feigned madness with Avimelekh,*
   who therefore sent him away, and he left.
   I bless You every moment *Adonai*—praise of You is always
       on my lips—
   In You, *Adonai,* my being revels.
   Hear and rejoice, fellow seekers,
   come and extol *Adonai* with me. Let us exalt the Holy One
       together!

5 I sought *Adonai,* and *Adonai* answered me and saved me
       from my worst terrors—
   Those who look to *Adonai* glow; never again do they
       pale with fear.
   A poor soul cried out, and *Adonai* heard, and rescued him
       from his troubles:
   Adonai sends an angel to protect the faithful, and the angel
       sets them free:

   O taste and see that *Adonai* is good! how happy are those
       who realize that!

10 O fill yourselves with awe for *Adonai,* you holy ones, and
       never again will you feel lack—
   young lions may suffer hunger and want,
   but seeking *Adonai,* you will have only good:
   Come, children, listen to me, I will teach you to feel awe of
       God.
   Which of you, yearning for life, would love long days of
       seeing only good?

PSALM 34 (Continued)

15 סוּר מֵרָע וַעֲשֵׂה־טוֹב בַּקֵּשׁ שָׁלוֹם וְרָדְפֵהוּ:

עֵינֵי יְהֹוָה אֶל־צַדִּיקִים וְאָזְנָיו אֶל־שַׁוְעָתָם:

פְּנֵי יְהֹוָה בְּעֹשֵׂי רָע לְהַכְרִית מֵאֶרֶץ זִכְרָם:

צָעֲקוּ וַיהֹוָה שָׁמֵעַ וּמִכָּל־צָרוֹתָם הִצִּילָם:

קָרוֹב יְהֹוָה לְנִשְׁבְּרֵי־לֵב וְאֶת־דַּכְּאֵי־רוּחַ יוֹשִׁיעַ:

20 רַבּוֹת רָעוֹת צַדִּיק וּמִכֻּלָּם יַצִּילֶנּוּ יְהֹוָה:

שֹׁמֵר כָּל־עַצְמוֹתָיו אַחַת מֵהֵנָּה לֹא נִשְׁבָּרָה:

תְּמוֹתֵת רָשָׁע רָעָה וְשֹׂנְאֵי צַדִּיק יֶאְשָׁמוּ:

פּוֹדֶה יְהֹוָה נֶפֶשׁ עֲבָדָיו וְלֹא יֶאְשְׁמוּ כָּל־הַחֹסִים בּוֹ:

PSALM 34 (*Continued*)

15 Keep your tongue from evil and your lips from lies— avoid
    evil and do good—
Seek peace and pursue it.

The eyes of *Adonai* are on the just; God's ears are open to
    their cry.
The face of *Adonai* is set against evil-doers, erasing the very
    thought of them from the world.
Cry out and *Adonai* hears, saving you from troubled straits
for *Adonai* is close to the heart-broken
and those whose spirits are crushed.

20 Good people suffer many troubles—but *Adonai* can soothe
    them,
protecting their very bones, not letting even one be broken
while evil kills off the evil, and the enemies of the good are
    doomed.
Adonai *redeems the life of the faithful:*
take shelter in God
and be safe.

PSALM 90

תְּפִלָּה לְמֹשֶׁה אִישׁ־הָאֱלֹהִים אֲדֹנָי מָעוֹן אַתָּה הָיִיתָ לָּנוּ 1
בְּדֹר וָדֹר:

בְּטֶרֶם הָרִים יֻלָּדוּ וַתְּחוֹלֵל אֶרֶץ וְתֵבֵל וּמֵעוֹלָם עַד־עוֹלָם
אַתָּה אֵל:

תָּשֵׁב אֱנוֹשׁ עַד־דַּכָּא וַתֹּאמֶר שׁוּבוּ בְנֵי־אָדָם:

כִּי אֶלֶף שָׁנִים בְּעֵינֶיךָ כְּיוֹם אֶתְמוֹל כִּי יַעֲבֹר
וְאַשְׁמוּרָה בַלָּיְלָה:

זְרַמְתָּם שֵׁנָה יִהְיוּ בַּבֹּקֶר כֶּחָצִיר יַחֲלֹף: 5

בַּבֹּקֶר יָצִיץ וְחָלָף לָעֶרֶב יְמוֹלֵל וְיָבֵשׁ:

כִּי־כָלִינוּ בְאַפֶּךָ וּבַחֲמָתְךָ נִבְהָלְנוּ:

שַׁתָּה עֲוֹנֹתֵינוּ לְנֶגְדֶּךָ עֲלֻמֵנוּ לִמְאוֹר פָּנֶיךָ:

כִּי כָל־יָמֵינוּ פָּנוּ בְעֶבְרָתֶךָ כִּלִּינוּ שָׁנֵינוּ כְמוֹ־הֶגֶה:

PSALM 90

1   *A prayer for Moses, a man of God:*
    Generation after generation, *Adonai,* You have been our
        refuge.
    Before the mountains were born, before the earth and the
        world itself
        writhed into life:
    forever and forever
    You have been God.

    But us You return to mere dust, as if saying
    "Go back to the earth, children of the earth."
    Though in Your eyes a thousand years are a fleeting
        yesterday,
    passing as if in a dream, we are like grass—

5   like grass that flourishes in the morning sun
    but by evening withers and dies.

    For it is Your anger that devours us, Your rage that fills us
        with terror.
    You lay out all of our faults, You shine Your light
    on our most secret sins. In the presence of Your anger, our
        days slip away—
    our whole lives seem no more than a whisper.

PSALM 90 (*Continued*)

10 יְמֵי שְׁנוֹתֵינוּ בָהֶם שִׁבְעִים שָׁנָה וְאִם בִּגְבוּרֹת שְׁמוֹנִים שָׁנָה

וְרָהְבָּם עָמָל וָאָוֶן כִּי־גָז חִישׁ וַנָּעֻפָה:

מִי־יוֹדֵעַ עֹז אַפֶּךָ וּכְיִרְאָתְךָ עֶבְרָתֶךָ:

לִמְנוֹת יָמֵינוּ כֵּן הוֹדַע וְנָבִא לְבַב חָכְמָה:

שׁוּבָה יְהוָה עַד־מָתָי וְהִנָּחֵם עַל־עֲבָדֶיךָ:

שַׂבְּעֵנוּ בַבֹּקֶר חַסְדֶּךָ וּנְרַנְּנָה וְנִשְׂמְחָה בְּכָל־יָמֵינוּ:

15 שַׂמְּחֵנוּ כִּימוֹת עִנִּיתָנוּ שְׁנוֹת רָאִינוּ רָעָה:

יֵרָאֶה אֶל־עֲבָדֶיךָ פָעֳלֶךָ וַהֲדָרְךָ עַל־בְּנֵיהֶם:

וִיהִי נֹעַם אֲדֹנָי אֱלֹהֵינוּ עָלֵינוּ וּמַעֲשֵׂה יָדֵינוּ כּוֹנְנָה עָלֵינוּ

וּמַעֲשֵׂה יָדֵינוּ כּוֹנְנֵהוּ:

PSALM 90 (*Continued*)

10   Our lives last for seventy years—and if we have strength,
         eighty.
      Most of them are hard work and sadness
      and pass by too quickly before we're cut down.
      The full force of Your anger is as immeasurable
      as the fear many feel toward You.

      Adonai, teach us how to make each of our days matter
      so that our hearts may become wise.
      Come back to us, *Adonai,*
      how long must we wait for Your compassion?
      Sate us with Your kindness every morning
      and our whole lives will brim with gladness and joy—

15   Give us joy equal to the sorrow we've suffered,
      the years we felt only pain.

      Let this, Your goodness, be revealed to all who pray to You,
      Let our children see Your glory.
      May we ourselves feel Your loveliness, *Adonai,* our God,
      and may the works of our own hands be realized,
      the works of our own hands realized.

PSALM 91: A PSALM OF TRUST

1   יֹשֵׁב בְּסֵתֶר עֶלְיוֹן בְּצֵל שַׁדַּי יִתְלוֹנָן:

אֹמַר לַיהוָה מַחְסִי וּמְצוּדָתִי אֱלֹהַי אֶבְטַח־בּוֹ:

כִּי הוּא יַצִּילְךָ מִפַּח יָקוּשׁ מִדֶּבֶר הַוּוֹת:

בְּאֶבְרָתוֹ יָסֶךְ לָךְ וְתַחַת כְּנָפָיו תֶּחְסֶה צִנָּה וְסֹחֵרָה אֲמִתּוֹ:

5   לֹא־תִירָא מִפַּחַד לָיְלָה מֵחֵץ יָעוּף יוֹמָם:

מִדֶּבֶר בָּאֹפֶל יַהֲלֹךְ מִקֶּטֶב יָשׁוּד צָהֳרָיִם:

יִפֹּל מִצִּדְּךָ אֶלֶף וּרְבָבָה מִימִינֶךָ אֵלֶיךָ לֹא יִגָּשׁ:

רַק בְּעֵינֶיךָ תַבִּיט וְשִׁלֻּמַת רְשָׁעִים תִּרְאֶה:

כִּי־אַתָּה יְהוָה מַחְסִי עֶלְיוֹן שַׂמְתָּ מְעוֹנֶךָ:

10   לֹא־תְאֻנֶּה אֵלֶיךָ רָעָה וְנֶגַע לֹא־יִקְרַב בְּאָהֳלֶךָ:

כִּי מַלְאָכָיו יְצַוֶּה־לָּךְ לִשְׁמָרְךָ בְּכָל־דְּרָכֶיךָ:

עַל־כַּפַּיִם יִשָּׂאוּנְךָ פֶּן־תִּגֹּף בָּאֶבֶן רַגְלֶךָ:

עַל־שַׁחַל וָפֶתֶן תִּדְרֹךְ תִּרְמֹס כְּפִיר וְתַנִּין:

כִּי בִי חָשַׁק וַאֲפַלְּטֵהוּ אֲשַׂגְּבֵהוּ כִּי־יָדַע שְׁמִי:

PSALM 91: A PSALM OF TRUST

1 One who dwells within God's shelter
lives in the Almighty's protective shadow.
I call *Adonai* "my haven and my strength,"
for, my God, I trust You.
God will save you from hunters' traps,
    from deadly plague,
and protect you, shelter you
under the shadow
of God's wing—
God, our shield, our armor, we trust You.

5 Have no fear of the terrors of night, of arrows that fly by
    day—
of pestilence stalking at dusk,
or the scourge that strikes at noon.
Though thousands fall at your side
and ten thousand at your right hand,
you will be safe.
Only look with your eyes—the destruction
of the wicked is what you will see.

10 No harm can befall you, no affliction
approach your home.
God commands angels to guard you
on all your paths—
to lift you up with their palms, lest you stumble on stones.
Even if you tread on lion and adder,
or trample a serpent or a lion cub—
God will say, "Because you have clung to me,
I will save you,
I will set you up high you, for you know My Name.

PSALM 91: A PSALM OF TRUST (*Continued*)

15 יִקְרָאֵנִי וְאֶעֱנֵהוּ עִמּוֹ אָנֹכִי בְצָרָה אֲחַלְּצֵהוּ וַאֲכַבְּדֵהוּ:

אֹרֶךְ יָמִים אַשְׂבִּיעֵהוּ וְאַרְאֵהוּ בִּישׁוּעָתִי:

PSALM 91: A PSALM OF TRUST (*Continued*)

15 Whoever calls me, I will answer,
     and remain by their side through times of trouble,
     I will draw you out of danger
     and honor you,
     sating you with length of days—
     revealing to you My power to save."

PSALM 135

1   הַלְלוּיָהּ הַלְלוּ אֶת־שֵׁם יְהֹוָה הַלְלוּ עַבְדֵי יְהֹוָה:

שֶׁעֹמְדִים בְּבֵית יְהֹוָה בְּחַצְרוֹת בֵּית אֱלֹהֵינוּ:

הַלְלוּיָהּ כִּי־טוֹב יְהֹוָה זַמְּרוּ לִשְׁמוֹ כִּי נָעִים:

כִּי־יַעֲקֹב בָּחַר לוֹ יָהּ יִשְׂרָאֵל לִסְגֻלָּתוֹ:

5   כִּי אֲנִי יָדַעְתִּי כִּי־גָדוֹל יְהֹוָה וַאֲדֹנֵינוּ מִכָּל־אֱלֹהִים:

כֹּל אֲשֶׁר־חָפֵץ יְהֹוָה עָשָׂה בַּשָּׁמַיִם וּבָאָרֶץ בַּיַּמִּים

וְכָל־תְּהוֹמוֹת:

מַעֲלֶה נְשִׂאִים מִקְצֵה הָאָרֶץ בְּרָקִים לַמָּטָר עָשָׂה

מוֹצֵא־רוּחַ מֵאוֹצְרוֹתָיו:

שֶׁהִכָּה בְּכוֹרֵי מִצְרָיִם מֵאָדָם עַד־בְּהֵמָה:

שָׁלַח אֹתוֹת וּמֹפְתִים בְּתוֹכֵכִי מִצְרָיִם בְּפַרְעֹה וּבְכָל־עֲבָדָיו:

10   שֶׁהִכָּה גּוֹיִם רַבִּים וְהָרַג מְלָכִים עֲצוּמִים:

לְסִיחוֹן מֶלֶךְ הָאֱמֹרִי וּלְעוֹג מֶלֶךְ הַבָּשָׁן וּלְכֹל מַמְלְכוֹת כְּנָעַן:

וְנָתַן אַרְצָם נַחֲלָה נַחֲלָה לְיִשְׂרָאֵל עַמּוֹ:

יְהֹוָה שִׁמְךָ לְעוֹלָם יְהֹוָה זִכְרְךָ לְדֹר־וָדֹר:

כִּי־יָדִין יְהֹוָה עַמּוֹ וְעַל־עֲבָדָיו יִתְנֶחָם:

PSALM 135

1   *Hallelu-Yah!*
   Praise the name *Adonai,*
   Praise, those who worship *Adonai,*
      who stand here in the house of *Adonai,*
      here in the courtyard of our God!
   Hallelu-Yah! for *Adonai* is good,
   Sing to God's name, for it is pleasant,
   for *Adonai* has chosen Jacob
      and Israel as the treasured one,

5   O, I know *Adonai* is great, our God so beyond all other
      gods.
   Adonai desires, then does, all: in the heavens and earth,
   in the seas, the ocean depths—
   gathering clouds from the ends of the earth,
      making lightning bolts when it rains
   unleashing the winds from their heavenly vaults.

   This God smote the firstborn of Egypt, human and beast;
   sent signs and wonders into the midst of Egypt, into
      Pharaoh's midst,
      and all his servants—

10 smote many nations and killed mighty kings—
      Siḥon, king of the Amorites; Og, king of Bashan—and all
      the kingdoms of Canaan,
   giving their lands to Israel as an inheritance,
   as an inheritance for the people of God.
   Adonai, Your name is forever
   Adonai, generation after generation, will remember You,
   For You, *Adonai,* are just with Your people,
   and show compassion
   to all who worship You.

PSALM 135 (*Continued*)

עַצַבֵּי הַגּוֹיִם כֶּסֶף וְזָהָב מַעֲשֵׂה יְדֵי אָדָם: 15

פֶּה־לָהֶם וְלֹא יְדַבֵּרוּ עֵינַיִם לָהֶם וְלֹא יִרְאוּ:

אָזְנַיִם לָהֶם וְלֹא יַאֲזִינוּ אַף אֵין־יֶשׁ־רוּחַ בְּפִיהֶם:

כְּמוֹהֶם יִהְיוּ עֹשֵׂיהֶם כֹּל אֲשֶׁר־בֹּטֵחַ בָּהֶם:

בֵּית יִשְׂרָאֵל בָּרְכוּ אֶת־יְהוָֹה בֵּית אַהֲרֹן בָּרְכוּ אֶת־יְהוָֹה:

בֵּית הַלֵּוִי בָּרְכוּ אֶת־יְהוָֹה יִרְאֵי יְהוָה בָּרְכוּ אֶת־יְהוָֹה: 20

בָּרוּךְ יְהוָֹה מִצִּיּוֹן שֹׁכֵן יְרוּשָׁלָ͏ִם הַלְלוּיָהּ:

PSALM 135 (*Continued*)

15 The idols of nations are silver and gold, wrought by human
        hands—
     They have mouths but cannot speak, they have eyes but
        cannot see:
     They have ears but cannot hear—nor can they breathe with
        their mouth.

     Their makers and those who trust in them are just like them.

     O house of Israel, bless *Adonai,*
     O house of Aaron, bless *Adonai*
     O house of Levi, bless *Adonai.,*
     All who believe in *Adonai,* bless *Adonai!*
     Blessed be *Adonai* dwelling in Jerusalem,
     on Zion.
     Hallelu-Yah!

PSALM 136

1   הוֹדוּ לַיהֹוָה כִּי־טוֹב כִּי לְעוֹלָם חַסְדּוֹ:

הוֹדוּ לֵאלֹהֵי הָאֱלֹהִים כִּי לְעוֹלָם חַסְדּוֹ:

הוֹדוּ לַאֲדֹנֵי הָאֲדֹנִים כִּי לְעוֹלָם חַסְדּוֹ:

לְעֹשֵׂה נִפְלָאוֹת גְּדֹלוֹת לְבַדּוֹ כִּי לְעוֹלָם חַסְדּוֹ:

5   לְעֹשֵׂה הַשָּׁמַיִם בִּתְבוּנָה כִּי לְעוֹלָם חַסְדּוֹ:

לְרֹקַע הָאָרֶץ עַל־הַמָּיִם כִּי לְעוֹלָם חַסְדּוֹ:

לְעֹשֵׂה אוֹרִים גְּדֹלִים כִּי לְעוֹלָם חַסְדּוֹ:

אֶת־הַשֶּׁמֶשׁ לְמֶמְשֶׁלֶת בַּיּוֹם כִּי לְעוֹלָם חַסְדּוֹ:

אֶת־הַיָּרֵחַ וְכוֹכָבִים לְמֶמְשְׁלוֹת בַּלָּיְלָה כִּי לְעוֹלָם חַסְדּוֹ:

10 לְמַכֵּה מִצְרַיִם בִּבְכוֹרֵיהֶם כִּי לְעוֹלָם חַסְדּוֹ:

וַיּוֹצֵא יִשְׂרָאֵל מִתּוֹכָם כִּי לְעוֹלָם חַסְדּוֹ:

בְּיָד חֲזָקָה וּבִזְרוֹעַ נְטוּיָה כִּי לְעוֹלָם חַסְדּוֹ:

לְגֹזֵר יַם־סוּף לִגְזָרִים כִּי לְעוֹלָם חַסְדּוֹ:

וְהֶעֱבִיר יִשְׂרָאֵל בְּתוֹכוֹ כִּי לְעוֹלָם חַסְדּוֹ:

15 וְנִעֵר פַּרְעֹה וְחֵילוֹ בְיַם־סוּף כִּי לְעוֹלָם חַסְדּוֹ:

לְמוֹלִיךְ עַמּוֹ בַּמִּדְבָּר כִּי לְעוֹלָם חַסְדּוֹ:

לְמַכֵּה מְלָכִים גְּדֹלִים כִּי לְעוֹלָם חַסְדּוֹ:

וַיַּהֲרֹג מְלָכִים אַדִּירִים כִּי לְעוֹלָם חַסְדּוֹ:

לְסִיחוֹן מֶלֶךְ הָאֱמֹרִי כִּי לְעוֹלָם חַסְדּוֹ:

PSALM 136

1   Praise *Adonai* Who is good for God's kindness is forever
Praise our God of gods for God's kindness is forever.
Praise our Ruler of rulers for God's kindness is forever.
Who alone works great wonders for God's kindness is
     forever

5   Who, in wisdom, made the heavens for God's kindness is
     forever
Who laid out earth on the waters for God's kindness is
     forever
Who made the great lights of the sky for God's kindness is
     forever
The sun, to rule the day for God's kindness is forever
The moon and stars, to rule the night for God's kindness is
     forever

10 Who smote the firstborn in ancient Egypt for God's kindness
     is forever
And brought out Israel from their midst for God's kindness is
     forever
With a strong hand and an outstretched arm for God's
     kindness is forever
And cut the Reed Sea into pieces for God's kindness is
     forever
brought the people Israel through it for God's kindness is
     forever

15 swept Pharaoh and his armies into the sea for God's
     kindness is forever
led the people in the desert for God's kindness is forever
conquered mighty kings for God's kindness is forever
Sihon, king of the Amorites for God's kindness is forever

PSALM 136 (*Continued*)

20   וּלְעוֹג מֶלֶךְ הַבָּשָׁן כִּי לְעוֹלָם חַסְדּוֹ:

וְנָתַן אַרְצָם לְנַחֲלָה כִּי לְעוֹלָם חַסְדּוֹ:

נַחֲלָה לְיִשְׂרָאֵל עַבְדּוֹ כִּי לְעוֹלָם חַסְדּוֹ:

שֶׁבְּשִׁפְלֵנוּ זָכַר־לָנוּ כִּי לְעוֹלָם חַסְדּוֹ:

וַיִּפְרְקֵנוּ מִצָּרֵינוּ כִּי לְעוֹלָם חַסְדּוֹ:

25   נֹתֵן לֶחֶם לְכָל־בָּשָׂר כִּי לְעוֹלָם חַסְדּוֹ:

הוֹדוּ לְאֵל הַשָּׁמָיִם כִּי לְעוֹלָם חַסְדּוֹ:

PSALM 136 (*Continued*)

20 Og, king of the Bashan for God's kindness is forever
Giving their land as an inheritance for God's kindness is
forever
An inheritance to Israel, God's servant for God's kindness is
forever
and remembered us in our distress for God's kindness is
forever
and rescued us from our oppressors for God's kindness is
forever

25 giving food to all who live for God's kindness is forever
Praise the God of heaven whose kindness is forever.

PSALM 33

1 רַנְּנוּ צַדִּיקִים בַּיהוָה לַיְשָׁרִים נָאוָה תְהִלָּה:

הוֹדוּ לַיהוָה בְּכִנּוֹר בְּנֵבֶל עָשׂוֹר זַמְּרוּ־לוֹ:

שִׁירוּ לוֹ שִׁיר חָדָשׁ הֵיטִיבוּ נַגֵּן בִּתְרוּעָה:

כִּי־יָשָׁר דְּבַר־יְהוָה וְכָל־מַעֲשֵׂהוּ בֶּאֱמוּנָה:

5 אֹהֵב צְדָקָה וּמִשְׁפָּט חֶסֶד יְהוָה מָלְאָה הָאָרֶץ:

בִּדְבַר יְהוָה שָׁמַיִם נַעֲשׂוּ וּבְרוּחַ פִּיו כָּל־צְבָאָם:

כֹּנֵס כַּנֵּד מֵי הַיָּם נֹתֵן בְּאֹצָרוֹת תְּהוֹמוֹת:

יִירְאוּ מֵיהוָה כָּל־הָאָרֶץ מִמֶּנּוּ יָגוּרוּ כָּל־יֹשְׁבֵי תֵבֵל:

כִּי הוּא אָמַר וַיֶּהִי הוּא־צִוָּה וַיַּעֲמֹד:

10 יְהוָה הֵפִיר עֲצַת גּוֹיִם הֵנִיא מַחְשְׁבוֹת עַמִּים:

עֲצַת יְהוָה לְעוֹלָם תַּעֲמֹד מַחְשְׁבוֹת לִבּוֹ לְדֹר וָדֹר:

אַשְׁרֵי הַגּוֹי אֲשֶׁר־יְהוָה אֱלֹהָיו הָעָם בָּחַר לְנַחֲלָה לוֹ:

מִשָּׁמַיִם הִבִּיט יְהוָה רָאָה אֶת־כָּל־בְּנֵי הָאָדָם:

מִמְּכוֹן־שִׁבְתּוֹ הִשְׁגִּיחַ אֶל כָּל־יֹשְׁבֵי הָאָרֶץ:

PSALM 33

1   Rejoice in *Adonai,* you loyal ones—
praising God delights the faithful.
Praise *Adonai* with the lyre,
with the ten-stringed harp sing to God!
Sing a new song, play well, with sounds of your deepest
    feeling!
For the word of *Adonai* is true, and God's actions in good
    faith always.

5   *Adonai* loves the right and the just—God's kindness fills the
    whole earth
The heavens were made with *Adonai's* word, and hosts of
    heavens by
the breath of God's mouth.
God gathered the sea water like a mound and stored the
    depths of the sea in vaults.

Let all the earth hold God in awe—let all who dwell on
    earth feel awe,
For God but spoke, and the world came to be; God
    commanded,
    and the world stood firm.

10 *Adonai* thwarts the counsel of nations, overturning peoples'
    designs—
But *Adonai's* counsel will endure forever,
and from generation to generation, the designs
of God's heart will forever last.
How happy is the nation whose god is *Adonai,*
the people God chose to give an inheritance.
From the heavens *Adonai* looks down
and sees all human beings,
from God's own dwelling place overseeing
all who live on earth.

PSALM 33 (*Continued*)

15 הַיֹּצֵר יַחַד לִבָּם הַמֵּבִין אֶל־כָּל־מַעֲשֵׂיהֶם:

אֵין הַמֶּלֶךְ נוֹשָׁע בְּרָב־חָיִל גִּבּוֹר לֹא־יִנָּצֵל בְּרָב־כֹּחַ:

שֶׁקֶר הַסּוּס לִתְשׁוּעָה וּבְרֹב חֵילוֹ לֹא יְמַלֵּט:

הִנֵּה עֵין יְהוָה אֶל־יְרֵאָיו לַמְיַחֲלִים לְחַסְדּוֹ:

לְהַצִּיל מִמָּוֶת נַפְשָׁם וּלְחַיּוֹתָם בָּרָעָב:

20 נַפְשֵׁנוּ חִכְּתָה לַיהוָה עֶזְרֵנוּ וּמָגִנֵּנוּ הוּא:

כִּי־בוֹ יִשְׂמַח לִבֵּנוּ כִּי בְשֵׁם קָדְשׁוֹ בָטָחְנוּ:

יְהִי־חַסְדְּךָ יְהוָה עָלֵינוּ כַּאֲשֶׁר יִחַלְנוּ לָךְ:

PSALM 33 (*Continued*)

15 God fashions all hearts—one and all—
and understands all their deeds.
A ruler is not rescued by a great army,
a hero is not rescued by great strength—
a horse cannot save you; its mighty strength
helps no one escape.
Look! *Adonai* watches over those who
yearn for God's kindness, those who hold God in awe—
that God may save them from death, and

20 in times of famine, sustain their lives.
Our souls wait for *Adonai,*
Who is our help and our shield.
For in God our hearts rejoice, in God's holy name
have we put our trust.
May your kindness, O *Adonai,* be upon us, for we have long
yearned for You.

CHAPTER ELEVEN

Reaping in Joy:

The Blessing After Meals

Traditionally chanted on Shabbat afternoon, as well as on both festivals and Shabbat as the prelude to *Birkat Hamazon*, the Blessing after Meals, Ps 126 is both evocative and elusive, apparently so simple, and yet so challenging. For at the heart of the psalm is a basic, disconcerting, question that every interpreter and translator has to confront. Just *when* is the "when" the psalm is describing? *When* were "we . . . like dreamers?" And what does the psalm mean by restoring Zion? *Which* restoration of Zion? Has the restoration even happened yet—is the psalm describing a past event or an event yet to take place?

All these questions arise because of the quirky nature of Hebrew verbs. There is no past, present, and future tense in biblical Hebrew in the same way as there is, for example, in modern English. As Robert Alter points out, "Given the fluidity of verb tenses in biblical poetry, there is disagreement as to whether the verbs are to be understood as past or future!"[19] Although whether a verb is past or future has not been particularly significant for many of the psalms of the liturgy that we discussed previously, it does matter a great deal for the prayer experience of Ps 126.

[19]Alter, *The Book of Psalms* (New York: Norton, 2007), p. 447 n1.

When the Stone edition, for example, translates the line "When *HaShem* will return the captivity of Zion, we will be like dreamers," it is suggesting that we are in exile, and Zion is now captive. Praying the psalm, then, we are called upon to ask ourselves what the state of exile means for us today, and equally, in what ways Zion is still "captive." Are we in spiritual exile? From what? And if we see ourselves still as a nation in exile, what is the relationship between "Zion" and the state of Israel?

B'kol Echad, the pamphlet of prayers, blessings, and songs distributed by the United Synagogue of Conservative Judaism, offers us a very different prayer context. Rather than an expression of painful yearning, the psalm, in this translation, describes a wondrous happening: "When the Lord brought the exiles back to Zion, We were as in a dream." Now we're led to ask ourselves *when* the "exiles" were brought back—after the destruction of the First Temple, when Cyrus the Persian gave permission to our ancestors to rebuild the Temple in Jerusalem, or in 1948, when, for the first time in nearly two thousand years, with the establishment of the state of Israel, the national homeland of the Jewish people was restored in the land of Zion? Is this a prayer about an ancient event, or an event in our own era? As we pray the psalm, are we expressing gratitude to God for ending the too-long, troubled exile of the Jewish people among the nations of the world?

Perhaps, though, the prayer at the heart of Ps 126 is not actually about a return from exile at all, but rather an expression of hope that someday the "fortunes" of Zion, along with the role of Zion in the world and its prosperity, *will* be restored. From this point of view, the psalm gives voice to how we *would* feel when *Adonai* restored those fortunes. "When the Lord restores the fortunes of Zion—we see it as in a dream"—translates the Jewish Publication Society *Tanakh*. Or "we should be like dreamers," as Robert Alter suggests. Alternatively, though, we may be praying for the "fortunes of Zion," but they've already been restored! "When the Lord restored the fortunes of Zion," translates the

Oxford Bible, "we were like those who dream."[20] The psalm becomes not a prayer of yearning, but an expression of gratitude, a remembrance of things past.

Amazing, isn't it, what the range of meanings—and thus the range of prayer experiences—can be for just the opening lines of a single psalm!

There is a very different way to approach Ps 126 as prayer-experience that I would like to suggest. To begin with, we need to ask ourselves what the superscription—the words "A song of ascents," means. I admit it—there's no incontrovertible evidence of that meaning either! But there are some evocative suggestions. The Mishnah tells us that the Levites sang the Songs of Ascent (Pss 120-134) during the intense, ecstatic, Festival of the Water Drawing at the end of Sukkot. "Whoever did not see the rejoicing at the Water Drawing, has never seen rejoicing in their life," says the Mishnah (BT Sukkot 51a-b). The pious would dance with flaming torches, and the Levites would blow their trumpets and play their harps, lyres, cymbals, and "countless" other musical instruments—as well as sing the "Songs of Ascents," standing on the fifteen steps leading from one courtyard to another, as water was fetched for the libations.

Why a water festival? Rabbi Akiva said that the celebration of water at the end of Sukkot was intended to remind the Holy One to send rain in the season to come—for Sukkot marks the end of summer and fall and the beginning of winter in *Eretz Yisrael*, the end of the dry season and the beginning of the season of rain. We add the prayer for rain now even in the modern liturgy. Anyone who has lived through a drought or the threat of drought knows:

---

[20]The versions are from: *B'kol Echad*, ed. Cantor Jeffrey Shiovitz (New York: United Synagogue of Conservative Judaism, 1986), p. 42; *The New Oxford Annotated Bible: New Revised Standard Version*, ed. Michael D. Coogan (Oxford: Oxford University Press, 2001), p. 888; Robert Alter, *The Book of Psalms*, p. 444; *Tanakh: The Holy Scriptures* (Philadelphia: Jewish Publication Society), p. 1264; and *The Stone Edition Tanach* (New York: Mesorah, 1996), p. 1551.

bountiful rain in its season means crops will flourish, our lakes, rivers, and streams will be renewed, and our lives will be marked by well-being.

Now we can look anew at the prayer experience at the heart of Ps 126. So rich is the psalm with suggestions of plenitude and the mention of joy, it is difficult to accept that captivity, exile, or grief have anything to do with it. For in the first stanza, we talk of laughter *filling* our mouths, of our tongues singing with joy. And then, in the second stanza, "songs of joy" and "singing with joy" are repeated, as if our joy is intensifying, as if this is a "song of ascent" in the sense that as we move through the psalm, we are being carried toward an even greater joy. Indeed, from the very outset of the psalm, as we move from line to line, it is as if we are moving on an ascending staircase—like the Levites in the Temple at the Water Drawing Festival. What is it to feel like a "dreamer?" It is to experience ecstasy; to feel your mouth filled with laughter and your tongue filled with joy. It is to imagine the nations of the world filled with awe at the bounty of God for the people Israel. And even more than that, for not only did the nations say it and not only did we hear it, but we also felt it ourselves, and gave voice to it ourselves. Laughing and singing, in the last line of the first stanza, it is we ourselves now saying, now speaking, of the great things God has done for us.

The second stanza returns us to the first line, but with a twist: we have moved from a restoration of Zion, to a call for a restoration of *our own* well-being. It sounds, at first, as if we are asking only for agricultural prosperity. But one of the most fundamental aspects of our tradition is the conviction that the fertility of the land of Israel is intimately connected to the spiritual condition of the people Israel, as the prophet Jeremiah proclaims:

> The One who scattered Israel will gather them,
> and will guard them as a shepherd his flock.
> They shall come and shout on the heights of Zion,
> Radiant over the bounty of *Adonai*—

> Over new grain and wine and oil . . .
> They shall fare like a watered garden
> And never languish again. (Jer 31:1–12)

The restoration and joy Ps 126 evokes is thus both spiritual and physical—a land and a people made whole and flourishing once more by a beneficent God. How fitting and profound, then, that we pray this psalm before reciting *Birkat Hamazon*, the Blessing after Meals, on Shabbat and festivals. I think the "homecoming" for which we are praying is not a return from exile; it's a homecoming to a state of well-being, at-homeness with both our earth and our God.

The first section of the psalm deals with the past.

The second is a prayer for the present.

Now, as we finish the Shabbat or festival meal, as we pray the psalm, we reenact the restoration of our fortunes. We describe water streaming over the dry soil, seeds being sown, the very sheaves of wheat being carried in joyful hands. Having just eaten the "grain and wine and oil" of our meal, it's as if we took the psalm one step further—the penultimate step. The final step will be the praying of the Blessing after Meals itself. For what we are acknowledging is that God heard our prayer for well-being and watered the earth. In partnership with the Holy One, the farmer sowed and reaped. The wheat became food and nourished us.

The circle of the psalm has been completed.

God, human beings, and the natural world are all in harmony.

Laughter fills our mouths; tongues sing with joy.

Life is as it should be.

Holy Reading: Psalm 126

Radiant Over the Bounty of Adonai

As the people stand at the Jordan, Moses vividly describes the land of Israel beckoning to them on the horizon. It's "a good land," he says "a land with streams and springs and fountains issuing from plain and hill, a land of wheat and barley, vines, figs, and pomegranates, a land of olive trees and honey," a land "where you will lack nothing. . . ." Psalm 126 celebrates our return to that land—along with the generosity of earth itself. It rejoices in the sheer plentitude and simplicity of life at its best: lush rains becoming desert streams; mouths filled with laughter; fields richly golden and alive with the glory of ripening grain. It is a world to feel utterly at home in, a world of well-being, bountiful, and beneficent.

> "And when you have eaten your fill," Moses continues, "bless *Adonai* your God for the good land *Adonai* has given you" (Deut 8:7–10).

Like the words of Moses, Psalm 126 sees the earth breathing in God's goodness and the streams flowing with the bounty of God: our land, our food, as a gift. The spiritual and earthly are not separate realms: every crust of bread is a miracle—most of all those crusts that have been hard won. Meditating on a line or lines of Psalm 126 offers us the opportunity to focus on the miracle of everyday life, on how the everyday is infused with the holy, the most mundane with the sacred; the never-to-be-taken-for-granted blessedness of laughter filling our mouths, and tongues singing with joy. And to feel gratitude for those miracles is to bring to life the words of Moses to our people, before he leaves us to climb Mount Pisgah:

> *Blessed be you in the city and you in the country. Blessed be the issue of your womb, the produce of your soil, the offspring of your cattle . . . the lambing of your flock . . . Blessed shall be your basket and your kneading bowl.* (Deut 28:3–5).

PSALM 126

שִׁיר הַמַּעֲלוֹת בְּשׁוּב יְהֹוָה אֶת־שִׁיבַת צִיּוֹן הָיִינוּ כְּחֹלְמִים: 1

אָז יִמָּלֵא שְׂחוֹק פִּינוּ וּלְשׁוֹנֵנוּ רִנָּה אָז יֹאמְרוּ בַגּוֹיִם הִגְדִּיל

יְהֹוָה לַעֲשׂוֹת עִם־אֵלֶּה:

הִגְדִּיל יְהֹוָה לַעֲשׂוֹת עִמָּנוּ הָיִינוּ שְׂמֵחִים:

שׁוּבָה יְהֹוָה אֶת־שְׁבִיתֵנוּ כַּאֲפִיקִים בַּנֶּגֶב:

הַזֹּרְעִים בְּדִמְעָה בְּרִנָּה יִקְצֹרוּ: 5

הָלוֹךְ יֵלֵךְ וּבָכֹה נֹשֵׂא מֶשֶׁךְ־הַזָּרַע בֹּא־יָבוֹא בְרִנָּה

נֹשֵׂא אֲלֻמֹּתָיו:

PSALM 126

1   *A song of ascent.*
    When *Adonai* restored Zion, we were like dreamers.
    Laughter filled our mouths and our tongues sang with joy.
    Then the nations of the world said, "*Adonai* has done great
        things for them!"
    Adonai did do great things for us—and we were glad.

    O *Adonai,* restore our well-being now, like streams that flow
    in the Negev.

5   So those who sow in tears will reap with songs of joy—
    and those who walk along weeping, bearing a bag of seeds
    will surely come home singing with joy, bearing sheaves.

CHAPTER TWELVE

For the Sake of My Comrades and Friends:

A Psalm for Peace

When God created the world, says the Zohar, God placed the waters of the ocean around the earth and in the heart of the inhabited world, God placed Jerusalem. For many Jews, it does feel as if Jerusalem is, still today, the center of the world—whether we are talking about *"Yerushalayim shel' ma'lah,"* heavenly Jerusalem, or the Jerusalem of everyday. When the state of Israel is threatened, when war comes, when terrorist bombs explode in the city's bustling downtown, Jews all over the world gather together, urgently reciting Ps 122. That is when Ps 122 feels most like a prayer coming from one's very soul, and the pain one feels for the disparity between the hope and the reality is most acute. And all the more so, if you do indeed have comrades and friends living there.

What an archetypal expression of the ancient Jewish experience the psalm is, moreover! We saw in the last chapter that one view of the "Songs of Ascent" (Pss 120-134) is that they were chanted by Levites as they stood on the fifteen steps between two of the Temple courtyards. Another view is that the "Songs of Ascent" were chanted by pilgrims as they climbed up the mountains to Jerusalem from all over Israel, to celebrate the three "pilgrimage festivals": Passover, the spring festival of liberation;

Shavuot ("Feast of Weeks"), the wheat harvest, later also associated with the Revelation of the Torah on Mount Sinai; and Sukkot ("Festival of Tabernacles"), the autumn harvest which ended with the ecstatic Festival of the Water Drawing and the beginning of the prayers for winter rain. It is certainly true that Ps 122 seems to be *that* kind of "Song of Ascent," for the psalm is about that very pilgrimage experience.

And at the same time as it so vividly depicts the ancient pilgrims on their way to Jerusalem, Ps 122 captures a very contemporary ache. For when has Jerusalem *ever* been tranquil? Generation after generation, since earliest times, the city has suffered invasions, destruction, neglect, division and divisiveness. Indeed, one of the painful ironies of the current situation is that, in ways that evoke the old pre-1967 Mandelbaum Gate, a fence again divides the city from the surrounding land.

But the wars within and around Jerusalem are also evidence of more profound divisions within us and in the world as a whole. To pray for the peace of Jerusalem is thus in a sense to pray for the whole world; not because Jerusalem *is* the world but because to achieve a true, full, peace for that long-troubled city would take such a revolution in human consciousness, all humanity would be affected. In that day, in the words of Micah (4:1-4),

> . . . the many nations shall go up and shall say
> "Come, let us go up to the Mount of *Adonai* . . .
> That we may be instructed in God's ways,
> And walk in God's paths. . . ."
> And they shall beat their swords into plowshares,
> and their spears into pruning hooks.
> Nation shall not take up sword against nation;
> they shall never again know war.
> Every one will sit under their vine and fig tree
> And no one will make them afraid."

Amen!

1 שִׁיר הַמַּעֲלוֹת לְדָוִד שָׂמַחְתִּי בְּאֹמְרִים לִי בֵּית יְהֹוָה נֵלֵךְ:

עֹמְדוֹת הָיוּ רַגְלֵינוּ בִּשְׁעָרַיִךְ יְרוּשָׁלָם:

יְרוּשָׁלַם הַבְּנוּיָה כְּעִיר שֶׁחֻבְּרָה־לָּהּ יַחְדָּו:

שֶׁשָּׁם עָלוּ שְׁבָטִים שִׁבְטֵי־יָהּ עֵדוּת לְיִשְׂרָאֵל לְהֹדוֹת

לְשֵׁם יְהֹוָה:

5 כִּי שָׁמָּה יָשְׁבוּ כִסְאוֹת לְמִשְׁפָּט כִּסְאוֹת לְבֵית דָּוִיד:

שַׁאֲלוּ שְׁלוֹם יְרוּשָׁלָם יִשְׁלָיוּ אֹהֲבָיִךְ:

יְהִי־שָׁלוֹם בְּחֵילֵךְ שַׁלְוָה בְּאַרְמְנוֹתָיִךְ:

לְמַעַן־אַחַי וְרֵעָי אֲדַבְּרָה־נָּא שָׁלוֹם בָּךְ:

לְמַעַן בֵּית־יְהֹוָה אֱלֹהֵינוּ אֲבַקְשָׁה טוֹב לָךְ:

PSALM 122

1 *A song of ascents, for David.*
   I rejoiced when they said to me, "Let us go to the House of
      Adonai!"
   Our feet were standing within your gates, Jerusalem—
      Jerusalem, built as a city bound together well—

5 It was there the tribes went— God's tribes—
   to fulfill laws of Torah by giving thanks to *Adonai*
   for there in Jerusalem the thrones of judgment stood,
   thrones of the house of David.

   Pray for the peace of Jerusalem,
   May those who love you feel tranquil!
   May there be peace within your ramparts,
   serenity in your citadels.
   For the sake of my comrades and friends,
   I pray for your peace—
   For the sake of the house of *Adonai* our God,
   I seek your good.

CHAPTER THIRTEEN

For You Are with Me:

Psalm 23

"An Ageless Comfort in Times of Pain," was the headline in the *Los Angeles Times*. "The 23rd Psalm, one of the most beloved passages in the Bible," said the sub-head, "offers solace to many people confronted by life's problems."[21] One woman, living with her husband's devastating illness, described the psalm as her "lifeblood"; the former music director of the Los Angeles Chorale, who had conducted countless musical settings for the psalm, said it "has everything you want in it. It gives you protection; it gives you solace. It gives you food."

At funerals and memorial (*Yizkor*) services, when we feel grief and loss more acutely, our liturgy offers us the twenty-third psalm for solace. Yet limiting the praying of the psalm to its liturgical context is a shame; it is there for us to draw on during the many moments and situations in our lives when we need solace.

What is it about this psalm that is so comforting?

To begin with, the psalm beckons us—who are so accustomed to seeing ourselves as "captains of our ship, masters of our fate," in charge of our own lives—to let go, to surrender the burden of, and our need for, control. *Let go, let God*, as a twelve-step program puts it. Because our Shepherd will lead us

---

[21]K. Connie Kang, August 9, 2003, B-22.

to "green pastures" and "still waters," we can follow safely: the
pasture is green— the world is alive; we will be nourished; we
will feel peaceful. We can follow; we don't have to lead. We can
be one of many; we need not stand out. At last, it is safe to be
. . . passive.

But there is nothing negative about the passivity honored in
the opening stanza of the psalm. Rather, that passivity is really a
yielding up of our ego. When we stop trying to exert control over
everything (and everyone?) around us, when, indeed, we "let Go,
and let God," our souls are restored. To allow yourself to be shep-
herded by God, by spiritual principles, by Torah, is to discover
that you are walking "in paths of righteousness," paths of just
behavior, of doing the right and the good. Just three lines—and
one of the most powerful descriptions of the nature and contours
of spiritual experience, of Torah living.

The second stanza of the psalm maps an even more profound
spiritual experience. To walk "in the valley of the shadow of
death," is to be human. Perhaps we are aware of it only when we
are ill, only when our well-being is threatened. But that is the
valley we are all walking in, all the time, whether we are aware of
it or not on a daily basis. What, given the nature of human life,
given the *brevity* of human life, can we do here on earth to feel
solace, to feel that our lives have meaning? I would like to suggest that the "table" that God sets up for us, in the face of our
"enemies"—in the face of all our fears, anxieties, worries, soul-
sapping concerns, whatever they may be, whoever our individual
"enemies" are—that "table" is the space for holiness that we
open within ourselves. It is in that inner space that we can discover both meaning and solace.

Each of us needs to imagine that table for ourselves.

When we allow ourselves fully to see it, fully to feel it, our
cup indeed "runneth over."

And then may we find ourselves truly dwelling in the house of
Adonai forever.

1   מִזְמוֹר לְדָוִד יְהֹוָה רֹעִי לֹא אֶחְסָר:

בִּנְאוֹת דֶּשֶׁא יַרְבִּיצֵנִי עַל־מֵי מְנֻחוֹת יְנַהֲלֵנִי:

נַפְשִׁי יְשׁוֹבֵב יַנְחֵנִי בְמַעְגְּלֵי־צֶדֶק לְמַעַן שְׁמוֹ:

גַּם כִּי־אֵלֵךְ בְּגֵיא צַלְמָוֶת לֹא־אִירָא רָע כִּי־אַתָּה עִמָּדִי

שִׁבְטְךָ וּמִשְׁעַנְתֶּךָ הֵמָּה יְנַחֲמֻנִי:

5   תַּעֲרֹךְ לְפָנַי שֻׁלְחָן נֶגֶד צֹרְרָי דִּשַּׁנְתָּ בַשֶּׁמֶן רֹאשִׁי כּוֹסִי רְוָיָה:

אַךְ טוֹב וָחֶסֶד יִרְדְּפוּנִי כָּל־יְמֵי חַיָּי וְשַׁבְתִּי בְּבֵית־יְהֹוָה

לְאֹרֶךְ יָמִים:

PSALM 23

1   *A song for David.*
      Adonai is my shepherd; I shall not want.
      God makes me lie down in green pastures and leads me beside
         the still waters,
      restoring my soul, leading me in the paths of righteousness
         for the Name's sake.

      Yea, though I walk through the valley of the shadow of
         death,
      I will fear no evil: for You are with me,
      Your rod and Your staff, they comfort me.
      You prepare a table before me in the presence of my
         enemies,
      You anoint my head with oil—
      My cup runneth over.

      Surely goodness and mercy shall follow me all the days of
         my life:
      and I will dwell in the house of *Adonai* forever.

Afterword

In the summer of '08, my family and I went on a kayaking and sailing adventure near southern California's Channel Islands. As we kayaked along the rocky shores of Anacapa Island, over vast underwater kelp forests, all around us were pelicans, seagulls, and cormorants perched on the rugged cliffs overlooking the sea. Harbor seals and sea lions lazed on the off-shore boulders and banks of sand, as splendidly-colored fish went darting about in the sea. Anacapa was brimming over with life.

The next day, as we sailed off the coast of Santa Barbara on a small ship, schools of dolphins swam alongside us, leaping from time to time in the air, hitching a ride on the water-stream set in motion by our boat. And then, suddenly, there they were: the largest, loudest, most thoroughly amazing mammals that have ever lived on the planet Earth: 80–90 foot-long Great Blue Whales!

Overwhelmed by all I was seeing and feeling, I found myself murmuring the joyous words of Psalm 104:

> How great are Your works, *Adonai*: You fashioned all life
>   with wisdom,
> The earth is filled with Your creation!
> Here is the sea, great and wide, where ships sail—
> It teems with creatures—small ones and large—
> There is the Leviathan You fashioned to frolic with!

When we hiked to the summit of Anacapa island, I half-expected to discover that the "cliffs of rock [sheltered] the little shrew mouse"!

I felt profoundly grateful to the psalmist who had first uttered those words, for they had given me a way to express my own sense of awe and joy at the vivid variety of sealife we had seen. At the same time knowing and being able to speak these lines had made the experience even richer for me, for the psalm had given me a language for my other inchoate, almost inexpressible, sense of spiritual wonder.

At emotionally fraught moments, how often do we find ourselves murmuring, with a certain reluctant frustration, "If I only had the words . . ."? How often, struggling to articulate what we're feeling, do we shrug our shoulders, almost sadly, and say, "Whatever . . ."? Yet there indeed *are* words available to us, words that articulate our deepest longings, our terrors, our ecstasy, our awe, our fear, our hope, our anger, our anxiety, our sense of justice, our gratitude, our moral commitment, our capacity to love: our relationship to our own innermost being, to other people, and to God. What I hope readers have discovered in *Psalms of the Jewish Liturgy* is that the language of the psalms gives us the words to articulate the variegated landscape of our own souls.

And more than articulate. For becoming familiar with the psalms can deepen, enrich, and illuminate our very experience itself, our grasp of those moments in our lives when our "cup runneth over," or, on the contrary, we feel as if we're "trembling with terror" or flooding our bed "with tears, every night" (Ps 23, Ps 6)—or aching for a sense of meaning:

> *Adonai*, teach us how to make each of our days matter
> so that our hearts may become wise. (Ps 90)

To speak those words, for example, is to be lifted out of a sense of isolation. It is to be tacitly connected to all those who, feeling those same feelings, have turned to those same words. How healing that sense of connection can be. How vital.

So now that you've finished reading the book, I hope you will go back, return to the psalms that drew you in, the ones that piqued your soul, or meant the most to you. I hope you will make those psalms your own beloved friends, part of the vocabulary of your own life. May you find the process of doing so "sweeter than honey from the honeycomb."

Sources

In the process of preparing the translations and the commentary, I consulted many sources. The first and most important source were the notes I took in Dr. Lieber's Psalms class at the American Jewish University. It was Dr. Lieber's emphasis on the structure of the individual psalms that opened my eyes to their poetic power in a new way.

Robert Alter's *The Book of Psalms: A Translation with Commentary* (New York: W. W. Norton, 2007), is a masterful work of scholarship and intellect from which I learned a great deal and upon which I often drew.

I found myself often turning to Martin S. Cohen's *Our Haven and Our Strength: The Book of Psalms* (New York: Aviv Press, 2004), for thought-provoking inspiration while wrestling with the meaning and implications of many of the psalms. Though at times our interpretations differ, Cohen's insights are frequently brilliant.

Reuven Hammer's *Or Hadash: A Commentary on Siddur Sim Shalom* (New York: Rabbinical Assembly, 2003), was for me a fount of knowledge.

Lawrence Kushner, *The Book of Letters* (Woodstock: Jewish Lights Publishing, 1990), has been a continued source of inspiration.

Mikra'ot Gedolot Hamalei המלא גדולות מקראות (Lakewood: Judaica Center, n.d.) was a vital resource for me, to see how our traditional commentators (Rashi, Ibn Ezra, Radak, Malbim, among others) interpreted both psalms as a whole and particular lines.

In the process of translating, I consulted the variant texts offered by *The New Oxford Annotated Bible*, ed. Michael D. Coogan, (Oxford: Oxford University Press, 2001); *The Authorized Daily Prayer Book Revised Edition*, ed. Joseph H. Hertz .New York: Bloch, 1948; *Tanakh: The Holy Scriptures, The New JPS Translation* (Philadelphia: Jewish Publication Society, 1988).

The *Renovare Spiritual Formation Bible: New Revised Standard Version*, ed. Richard J. Foster (San Francisco: Harper, 1989), while intended for Christians, inspires my whole approach to the psalms, and reminds me how much we Jews can learn from Christian spirituality and their understanding of the spiritual disciplines.

List of Abbreviations

BT	Babylonian Talmud
Exod	Exodus
Gen	Genesis
Jer	Jeremiah
1–2 Kgs	1–2 Kings
Sifre Deut	Sifre Deuteronomy
Zekh	Zekhariah

Miriyam Glazer, a Conservative rabbi, Professor of Literature, and Chair of Communication Arts at American Jewish University, is the author of *Dreaming the Actual: Contemporary Fiction and Poetry by Israeli Women Writers*, and *Dancing on the Edge of the World: Jewish Stories of Faith, Inspiration, and Love*, and editor of *The Bedside Torah: Wisdom, Visions, and Dreams*.